Jackets, Coats and Suits

from *Threads*

Jackets, Coats and Suits

from *Threads*

The Taunton Press

Cover photo by Susan Kahn (fashion photo by Yvonne Taylor)

© 1992 by The Taunton Press, Inc.
All rights reserved.

First printing: November 1992
Printed in the United States of America

A THREADS Book

THREADS® is a trademark of The Taunton Press, Inc.,
registered in the U.S. Patent and Trademark Office.

The Taunton Press
63 South Main Street
Box 5506
Newtown, CT 06470-5506

Library of Congress Cataloging-in-Publication Data

Jackets, coats, and suits from Threads magazine.
    p.   cm.
    "A Threads book"—T.p. verso.
    Includes index.
    ISBN 1-56158-048-1
    1. Tailoring. 2. Tailoring (Women's) 3. Coats. I. Threads magazine
TT580.J27 1992   92-30693
    646.4'3304—dc20   CIP

Contents

Introduction

So you've taken the leap and are going to sew a jacket, but you don't have much time. Maybe you've already made several suits, but you're looking for more polish. Where can you find the information you need?

Threads, naturally. This collection of articles from the past several years of *Threads* magazine, written by expert tailors, dressmakers, patternmakers and editors, offers advice and techniques to help you make some of the critical sewing and tailoring choices. You'll find out about options in style and cut—from a traditional tweed overcoat to a softly tailored Giorgio Armani jacket or a timeless Issey Miyake folded wonder. You'll also learn how to prepare and work with classic fabrics and contemporary interfacings, including gabardines and time-saving fusibles—and about details that give a garment that professional look, such as couture lapels, easy-to-construct sleeve vents, machine-sewn linings, and welt pockets that you can reach from inside or out.

And if you're looking for a simple casual coat, we've included a bonus pattern by American designer Bonnie Cashin.

—*Amy T. Yanagi, executive editor*

Inside an Armani Jacket
Exploring the secrets of the Master of Milan

by Ann Hyde

in 1974, an unknown named Giorgio Armani burst upon the fashion scene with an unconstructed blazer that changed forever the way women could look in suits. Today Armani is a major fashion force throughout the world, and his trademark remains unchanged: top-quality traditional men's tailored jackets remade for a woman's body. The key to the transformation was then, and is still, to soften and reduce the internal structure while preserving all the subtlety of the original cut, and then to make the resulting garment in women's sizes and in extraordinary and sensuous fabrics. The idea is simple; the trick is to know how to carry it off.

Armani has carried the idea off so well that his entirely machine-made jackets have achieved nearly legendary levels of desirability; they sell briskly despite prices in the neighborhood of $1000 and up a piece. I recently had the opportunity to closely examine a dozen or so begged and borrowed Armani jackets, from this and previous seasons. I swooned over the fabrics, analyzed the cut, and explored the inner workings to my heart's content, and confirmed that no matter how far he appears to stray, Armani has kept steadfastly to his roots in traditional Italian tailoring. He has simply pared his garments down to their essentials as he refines his own vision of comfortable sophistication.

For example, this spring Armani pulled virtually every scrap of interfacing out of his flagship jackets, like the one at right. But somehow the magic remains, proving beyond any doubt that the tailor's art is not just a matter of padding. It's all in the lines of an exquisitely drawn pattern, cut out in fabric equal to the task. But before we look more closely at how the Armani magic works, let's see where it all comes from.

Armani's menswear background

Unlike most designers of women's clothes, Armani's early fashion experience was gained designing menswear, and his impact here was revolutionary as well. Nino Cerruti, an Italian menswear manufacturer, hired him to design a new men's fashion line. Reacting against generations of stiff formality in men's suits, Armani lowered the lapels and buttons, took out padding, and softened the outline; his new jackets appeared, frankly, baggy—but it was a precise, sophisticated, and expressive sort of baggy, and men are still buying it today.

Armani struck out on his own in 1970 and struggled for four years exclusively with menswear while laboring to define his feminine silhouette. Eventually, he realized he needed to look no further than his own proven expertise. Armani himself acknowledges, "My first jackets for women were in fact (my) men's jackets in women's sizes" (*Time*, April 5, 1982, p. 63).

The basic ingredients

Among Armani's early training assignments with Cerruti was a stint in the mills. It was there, Armani has said, that he fell into a lifelong love affair with textiles and learned to appreciate what they could (or could not) do. In particular he learned that the soft lines he demanded in his jackets were achievable only with the finest quality fabrics.

Since those days Armani has always regarded the choice of fabric as critical. His

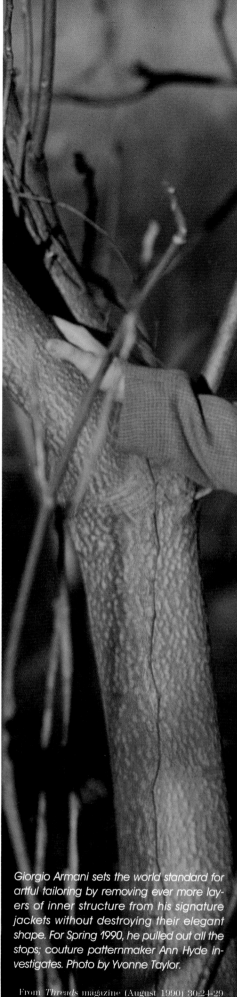

Giorgio Armani sets the world standard for artful tailoring by removing ever more layers of inner structure from his signature jackets without destroying their elegant shape. For Spring 1990, he pulled out all the stops; couture patternmaker Ann Hyde investigates. Photo by Yvonne Taylor.

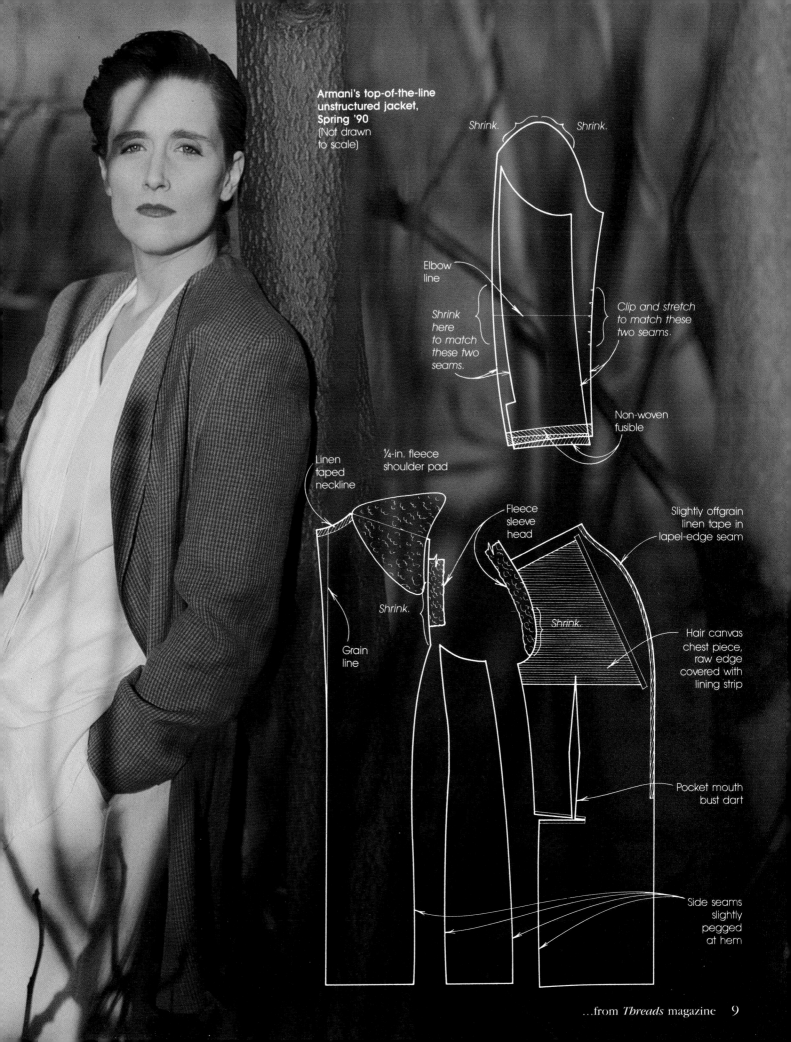

Armani's top-of-the-line unstructured jacket, Spring '90
(Not drawn to scale)

Shrink.   *Shrink.*

Elbow line

Shrink here to match these two seams.

Clip and stretch to match these two seams.

Non-woven fusible

Linen taped neckline

¼-in. fleece shoulder pad

Fleece sleeve head

Slightly offgrain linen tape in lapel-edge seam

Shrink.

Shrink.

Grain line

Hair canvas chest piece, raw edge covered with lining strip

Pocket mouth bust dart

Side seams slightly pegged at hem

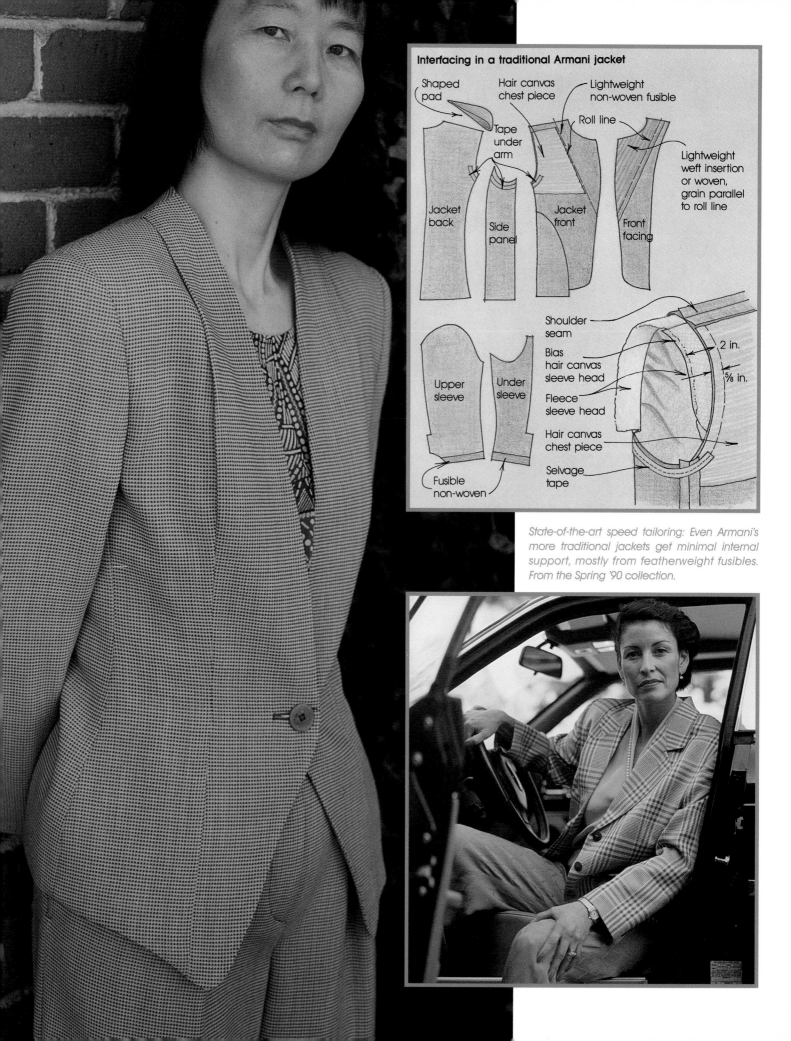

Interfacing in a traditional Armani jacket

Shaped pad

Hair canvas chest piece

Lightweight non-woven fusible

Roll line

Tape under arm

Jacket back

Side panel

Jacket front

Front facing

Lightweight weft insertion or woven, grain parallel to roll line

Shoulder seam

Bias hair canvas sleeve head

Fleece sleeve head

Hair canvas chest piece

Selvage tape

2 in.

⅝ in.

Upper sleeve

Under sleeve

Fusible non-woven

State-of-the-art speed tailoring: Even Armani's more traditional jackets get minimal internal support, mostly from featherweight fusibles. From the Spring '90 collection.

preference is a soft, natural-fiber, almost loosely-woven fabric, like the linens, wools, and rayons he used in the Spring '90 jackets shown here. He's not afraid of blends, like linen or wool with a little rayon, and seems particularly fond of very subtle texture; several of the fabrics for 1990 were almost waffle weaves, on the smallest scale. Because he subtracts the underpinnings, his fabrics must also be of stand-alone quality, capable of expressing his message without stiffeners or backing. Such fabrics are never inexpensive, and Armani's are almost always custom runs, full of exclusive detail, and in short supply.

Fabrics of this quality are certainly available to home sewers, especially in the major cities, but not without careful searching, a little luck, and a substantial budget. Most sewers would probably find, as I did, that a visit to an Armani boutique is a revelation, even if all they do is feel the fabrics; short of owning a closetful of his clothes, it's the best way to experience Armani's exquisite fabric judgment.

Color is of course a critical ingredient of Armani's formula. His definition of femininity demanded soft, subtle, and pale hues from the start. He'll alter his preferences from one season to the next—gray and ivory one season, earth tones the next—but his basic palette is always neutral, and rich, glowing with quality. The submissiveness of his background colors make drama from whatever accent pieces are worn, but the cumulative effect of an Armani ensemble is often such a triumph of minimalism that accessories become redundant.

About interfacings

For years I've been curious to know how Armani uses interfacings to achieve his unique fluidity, so I looked eagerly at two types of garments, both from the Spring '90 collection. I knew there would be fusibles in even his most expensive jackets, and I was right, but Armani still uses a few traditional materials. His approach seems to be "whatever works", with no particular value assigned to sewn-in materials. But like any manufacturer he can of course specify exactly what he wants from his fusible supplier and can apply it with specialized equipment for optimum results. I still shudder to think of fusing to a piece of $100-a-yard fabric, but Armani has given me new courage.

Minimal—Armani's more traditional garments, like the plaid jacket inset at left, and others with and without collars and lapels, like the one at far left, are made with a combination of woven and non-woven fusibles, with sewn-in chest pieces and sleeve heads, as shown in the drawing on

the facing page. The jacket front is fused almost entirely to a lightweight non-woven, like the lightest Pellon, except in the area between the pocket and side seam, just as you've been warned against doing in countless books and classes on using fusibles. There's no show-through on the front because the interfacing is so thin.

The chest piece is a single layer of very light, probably synthetic, hair canvas, barely stitched to the fusible underneath along the roll line and caught in the armhole seam at the other side, but stopping short of the shoulder seam; the top and bottom edges are free.

If the jacket has a lapel, the lapel area of the front facing is fused with an extremely light weft-insertion interfacing, from lapel edge to about an inch beyond the roll line, and with the grain parallel to it. The only commercially available material I've seen that comes close to the gauzy fabric Armani used is called Silkweight. It's a sheer, all-cotton woven fusible available from the Fabric Carr (Box 32120, San Jose, CA 95152-2120, 408-929-1651). They also sell a light-weight hair canvas like the one described above.

The jackets with collars are notable first for the separate stand and collar construction, shown in the photo below. These seem to me to have been cut primarily to reduce the amount of shaping with an iron that a traditional one-piece collar requires, replacing it with a shaped seam, as you can see in the drawing below. Under and upper collar

both have separate stands and are assembled, then joined, and pressed into shape. The upper collar and stand are each fused separately with a lightweight ongrain woven; the under collar is fused with a slightly heavier bias woven, but its stand is interfaced with a non-woven for a little more body.

The shoulder pads in these more traditional garments are custom-shaped foam (similar pads, called molded raglans, are available from G-Street Fabrics, 11854 Rockville Pike, Rockville, MD 20852, 301-231-8998) no more than a ½ in. thick, with substantial caps extending almost 2 in. into the sleeve to ensure that the cap shaping is perfect. In addition, each sleeve head is supported with a 2-in. wide strip of synthetic fleece that extends from just above the side panel seam in the back of the armscye to about an inch above the corresponding seam in the front, where the end of the fleece is trimmed to curve into the armscye, as in the drawing on p. 10. One jacket, from slightly heavier fabric, had in addition a bias-cut strip of traditional hair canvas included in the sleeve head seam underneath the fleece, from the shoulder seam to about the point of the front armscye notch, where it tapered to a point, like the fleece on top of it. The armscye seam is taped with a bit of lining selvage from notch to notch, in the underarm.

The only other area Armani chose to interface in these garments (all of which were from his white-label, mid-priced line) is the

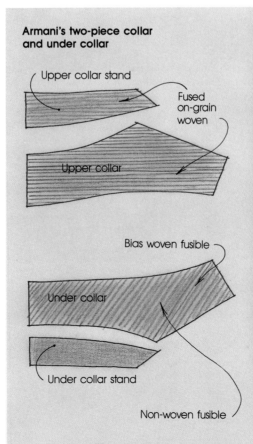

Armani's two-piece collar and under collar

Upper collar stand

Fused on-grain woven

Upper collar

Bias woven fusible

Under collar

Under collar stand

Non-woven fusible

For his mid-priced line, Armani cuts a separate stand for both collar and undercollar, eliminating time-consuming shaping of a one-piece collar with an iron.

sleeve hem, which he stiffened slightly with a 1-in. strip of non-woven fusible.

Sub-minimal — For at least one of his top-of-the-line (black-label) garments (the one shown on p. 9). Armani chose only sew-in interfacing (except for the merest strip of non-woven fusible in the sleeve hems, as before) in order to achieve a completely unstructured look. As you can see in the accompanying drawing, there's nothing inside this ultralight creation but a chest piece of traditional hair canvas, shaped and held just like the one described above, a ¼-in. thick fleece shoulder pad, and a fleece sleeve head the same shape and length as above. There's a thin strip of lining covering the raw edge at the front of the canvas, and a ¼-in. wide strip of just-offgrain linen-like fabric sewn into the shawl lapel, holding the edge firmly but permitting a little flex, and the back edge of the neckline is held with linen-like tape, and that's it. This jacket's secrets are all on the outside; let's take another look.

Cutting a masterpiece

By carefully following the woven check I could always locate the grain of the ultra-light jacket, making it easy to see the actual shape and orientation of seam lines. Starting at the back, I discovered that Armani had spread the jacket's shoulders not by cutting wider at the shoulders, but by adding a wedge from neck to back vent in the center. This turned out to be the case on every jacket I examined; you can see it clearly in the large plaid of the jacket shown above. Besides adding width gradually along the entire back above the hips (or above the waist in shorter jackets) this strategy lowers the shoulder line and softens the back's drape by throwing the fabric slightly offgrain.

Armani cut the back armscye seams almost exactly ongrain, but because of the center-back shaping these now hang at a slight angle; he's provided stability for the seam itself, and extra width for the boxy drape he wants at the bottom of the arms-cye. Following the shaping of the back/side-panel seam down from the armscye reveals that the back tapers sharply to the waist, bows outward slightly for the hips, then almost imperceptibly tapers back to peg the hemline. By adding such subtle movement (think in eighths of an inch) to jacket pattern seams that are essentially straight, as on most commercial patterns,

Every Armani jacket Hyde examined was cut with the center back spread off-grain to widen and lower the shoulders. Following the grain line along seams gives an immediate clue to the seam's shape.

you can greatly increase the finished garment's figure-enhancing impact.

Working from the top down in front, the deeply curved armscye is characteristic of the European/Italian tradition of high, snug-fitting sleeves. Look for similar armscyes on European patterns, like Burda. Compared to a typical American pattern, this armscye is simultaneously shorter (fits higher under the arm, and lower at the shoulder, with much less padding), wider (cuts more deeply into the jacket front, even though it's slightly flatter in back), and angled more towards the front, as you can see in the drawing on p. 9. The sleeve that fits this armscye is relatively narrow, with a shorter cap than the typical American pattern.

Further scrutiny of Armani's jacket reveals that the circumference of sleeve and armscye are virtually the same. The sleeve is eased at the cap, and the armscye is eased at both front and back curve in the bodice, to conform to the pectoral swell in front and the shoulder blade in back. I'd guess that this very slight sleeve and body shaping is done entirely without pressing; Armani's skilled machine operators can ease one layer to another, as they're sewing the layers together, with great precision.

Tailors typically shrink the roll line of a fitted jacket with an iron to shape it over the bust line; Armani opts for looseness and slouch in the drape of the lapel by eliminating this shaping. His jacket hangs open and loose at the buttoned waist, which is set set

lower than usual, all by design.

To continue shaping the jacket at the sides and under the bust (emphasizing the lack of shaping at the center front), Armani reverts to a subtle device straight out of the finest men's tailoring. If you look carefully at the grain lines above the pocket mouth in the close-up on p. 13, you'll see that they dip down toward the pocket, from the bust dart to the side panel seam. The pocket mouth is actually a continuation of the bust dart in this area, and not a mere slash in the jacket front; you can see the pattern shape in the drawing on p. 13. When the dart at the pocket is closed (the raw edges are butted together and zigzagged, not over-lapped), the entire side of the jacket front from the armscye under the bust to the waist is pulled slightly in, defining the bust and molding to the waist at the same time. Below the pocket, the side panel seam echoes the gentle hip and hem shaping we discovered in the back.

If you enjoy pattern manipulating (and the experimenting that it implies) you can try adding your own shaping to a pattern with a side panel and a vertical bust dart ending at the pocket. Make a tracing of the pattern and slash through the pocket mouth and up to the point of the bust dart, as in the drawing on the facing page, then fold out about a ¼-in. dart near the bottom of the armscye. This will rotate the pattern and open the pocket mouth. You may have to stretch this seam slightly to put the ¼ in. back into the armscye length.

Examining the sleeves confirmed that Armani had not neglected to shape them as well. As in traditional custom tailoring, the sleeve pieces curve gracefully around the arm because the top sleeve seamlines are cut to slightly different lengths than the corresponding undersleeve seams. In front, the top seam is shorter (about ⅜ in.) than the under seam, and in back the topseam is cut the same amount longer. By careful stretching and ease stitching, the seams are made to match again, and the sleeve curves more beautifully around the elbow.

Shaping fabric with an iron

The traditional method of shrinking and stretching fabric with heat, steam, and pressure is well within the grasp of the careful home sewer, and is the easiest way to bring some of Armani's subtlety to your projects. To shape the sleeve pieces and the armscye seams as described, as well as to shrink the sleeve cap to fit the armscye, I use a padded sleeve board and a Curity cloth diaper (available in discount stores and some pharmacies), half of which is dampened; the other half is dry. With my iron set to wool, I check the dampness. If the iron sizzles, the diaper's too wet, and I iron the diaper to dry it a bit.

To shrink the fabric near a seam, I first gather or ease-stitch the seam to the finished length I need. For the seam at the back of the sleeve (1½ in. either side of the elbow line), and at the armscye front and back, I ease-stitch as I make the seam.

Once the seam is gathered or stitched to the right length, I press only on the wrong side of the fabric, and only in the area within ⅜ in. of the seam. I lay the damp half of the diaper over the seam and press lightly with just the tip of the iron without any side-to-side motion, which would only stretch the seam. When the wrinkles or gathers are gone, I press dry with the other half of the press cloth to set the shrinkage.

After shrinking the armscye to its finished size, I machine stitch gathering rows on the sleeve cap from about 2½ in. either side of the center up to ⅜ in. from center; the ¾ in. in the middle shouldn't be gathered. With the sleeve pinned in place on the jacket (which should be on a form) I pull on the gathering threads until the cap matches the armscye and tie them off.

To stretch the front seam of the top sleeve, I clip into the seam allowance at an angle, staying two threads away from the seam line, and starting at the elbow line. I clip again 1½ in. on either side, then again between each clip. Then I start pressing the seam allowance from either end towards the middle, stretching as I go until the top sleeve matches the under sleeve, always working on the wrong side, and using the damp press cloth.

Do Armani's tailors go to these lengths with a hand iron on clothes that are entirely machined together? I can't say exactly how they do it, but the shaping is there, and it only confirms the fact that these garments have been stripped only to the essentials and not beyond. Armani's genius as a craftsman lies in knowing where to stop.   □

Ann Hyde is the founder of the Ann Hyde Institute of Design. She studied at the Chambre Syndical de la Couture Parisienne in France. For information about her summer workshops, phone (303) 355-1655 or write the Institute at P.O. Box 61271, Denver, CO 80222.

Thanks to Giorgio Armani Corp., New York, and Perkins Shearer and Lawrence Covell of Denver, CO, for their generous loan of sample garments.

Adding bust dart shaping to a pattern with a side panel

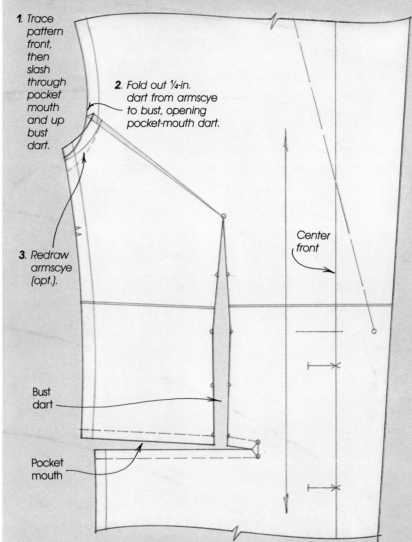

1. Trace pattern front, then slash through pocket mouth and up bust dart.

2. Fold out ¼-in. dart from armscye to bust, opening pocket-mouth dart.

3. Redraw armscye (opt.).

Center front

Bust dart

Pocket mouth

The angled grain above the pocket between the bust dart at right and the side panel seam at left reveals a concealed dart, hidden in the slash of the double welt pocket. The dart provides shaping under the bust and along the side seam.

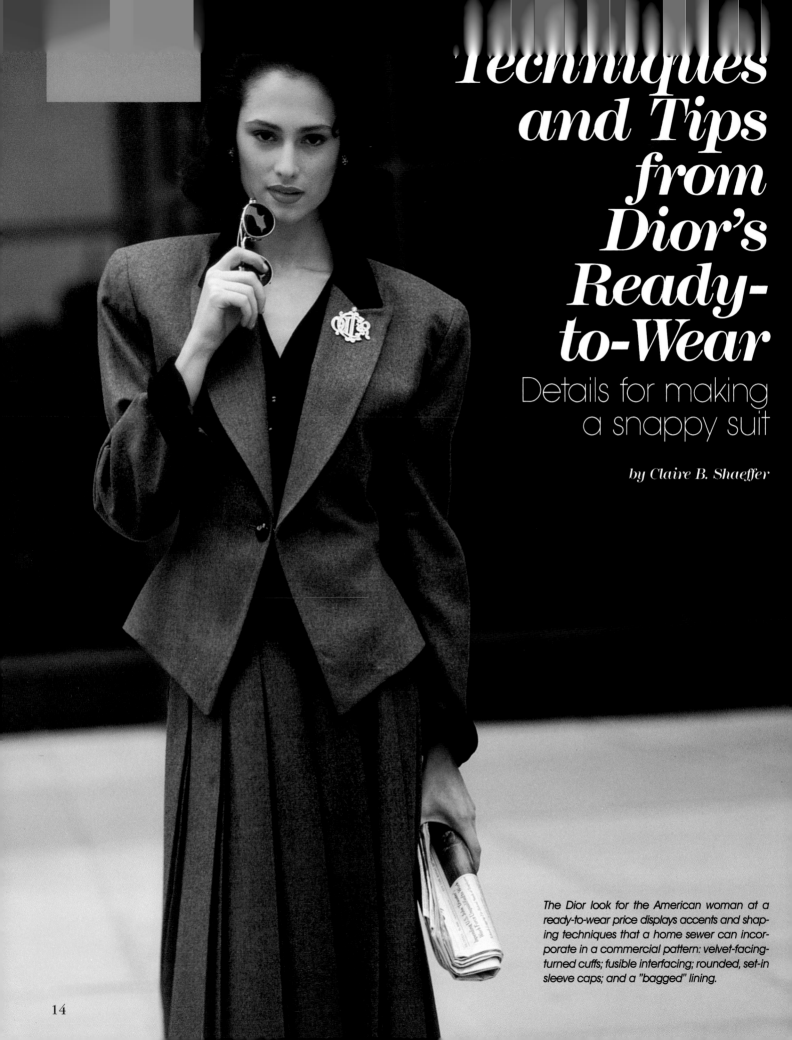

Techniques and Tips from Dior's Ready-to-Wear

Details for making a snappy suit

by Claire B. Shaeffer

The Dior look for the American woman at a ready-to-wear price displays accents and shaping techniques that a home sewer can incorporate in a commercial pattern: velvet-facing-turned cuffs; fusible interfacing; rounded, set-in sleeve caps; and a "bagged" lining.

if you've ever wanted to take a close look inside a particularly fine ready-to-wear garment, make yourself comfortable. I recently had the opportunity to examine the three-piece Christian Dior suit in the photo at left. Each piece–gray wool-flannel jacket, knife-pleated skirt, and cotton-velvet vest–can be worn separately. Appropriate to wear from the work place to dinner, the suit is an example of American ready-to-wear at its best and has excellent technical points that the home sewer can duplicate.

The suit, which retails for $500, was designed by Joyce Dixon for Christian Dior-The Suit, a licensee of Christian Dior, especially for the American customer for the current fall/winter season. The semifitted princess-line jacket, of good-quality, medium-weight wool flannel, skims the body gracefully from the shoulders to the waist before flaring into an attractive peplum, a result of the front section being cut with a definite flare (drawing at right). The box pleat in the back is a decorative detail. Velvet trim, a favorite fashion touch in this year's garments, is applied at the collar and turned-back cuffs and is easy to add to a standard jacket pattern. Underlining and interfacing, both fusible synthetics and woven cotton, ensure that the jacket's crisp, yet feminine, appearance remains even with long-term wear. A taped armscye, a sleeve head in the sleeve cap, and a hand-tacked raglan shoulder pad keep each shoulder gracefully round, yet firm.

The jacket lining, which reveals further quality workmanship, smoothly fits the inside of the jacket. Even though the shoulder pads are thick, no excess lining bunches at the shoulders. The lining was almost entirely machine-sewn into the jacket with a technique called "bagging," a much faster method than hand-slipstitching.

The skirt displays one of the most interesting features; the pleats have double knife edges that lie beautifully closed and flat. It's easier to have the pleats set commercially after you've stitched one side seam and hemmed the fabric to the final length, but you can also set them yourself.

A tailored look for a long time

Wool flannel drapes nicely but lacks the body to maintain this suit's crisp silhouette, so the jacket front and side panels were underlined with a medium-weight, fusible weft-insertion interfacing similar to Armo Weft (drawing at right).

If you use this trick, cut the underlining ¼ in. smaller than the shell fabric, and fuse it in place before stitching the darts and seams. Both the seams and darts in the Dior suit were clipped and pressed so well that from the outside of the garment

there's no indication that the interfacing has been stitched into the seamlines. Seams at the edges were trimmed, graded, and clipped to reduce the bulk.

Fusible knit interfacing, similar to Pellon's Knit Shape, was applied over the weft-insertion to interface the front shoulders, which keeps the jacket from collapsing over the hollow between the shoulder and bust. Knit interfacing is much softer than weft-insertion interfacing and adds a light touch. The same knit was also used to underline the velvet upper collar, the velvet cuffs, and the lapel facing.

As is common in custom suits but unusual in ready-to-wear, the upper part of the Dior jacket back is interfaced with wi-

gan, a cotton fabric similar to muslin but more firmly woven. Wigan is generally available from tailoring suppliers. When sewn into the seams, it maintains the shape of the armscyes, neckline, and shoulder areas and prevents the shoulder pad's shape from showing to the outside through the soft flannel. Preshrunk muslin would also work.

The wigan was cut in two pieces with a ½-in. overlap at the center back; I sometimes prefer an overlap of up to 2 in. so the wigan can be deeper at the center back. If the underarm panel isn't underlined, extend the wigan 2 in. below the armscye.

Since the back has no underlining, the back hem allowance was interfaced with a strip of bias-cut wigan. The wigan adds body

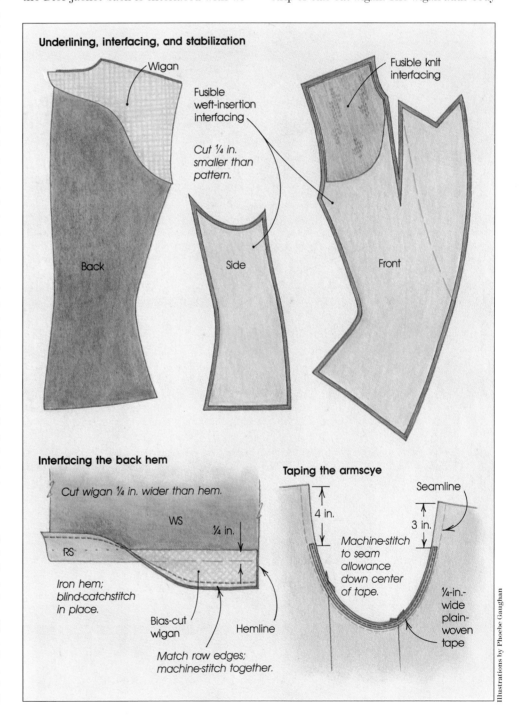

Underlining, interfacing, and stabilization

Wigan

Fusible weft-insertion interfacing

Cut ¼ in. smaller than pattern.

Fusible knit interfacing

Back

Side

Front

Interfacing the back hem

Cut wigan ¼ in. wider than hem.

WS

¼ in.

RS

Iron hem; blind-catchstitch in place.

Bias-cut wigan

Hemline

Match raw edges; machine-stitch together.

Taping the armscye

Seamline

4 in.

3 in.

Machine-stitch to seam allowance down center of tape.

¼-in.-wide plain-woven tape

Illustrations by Phoebe Gaughan

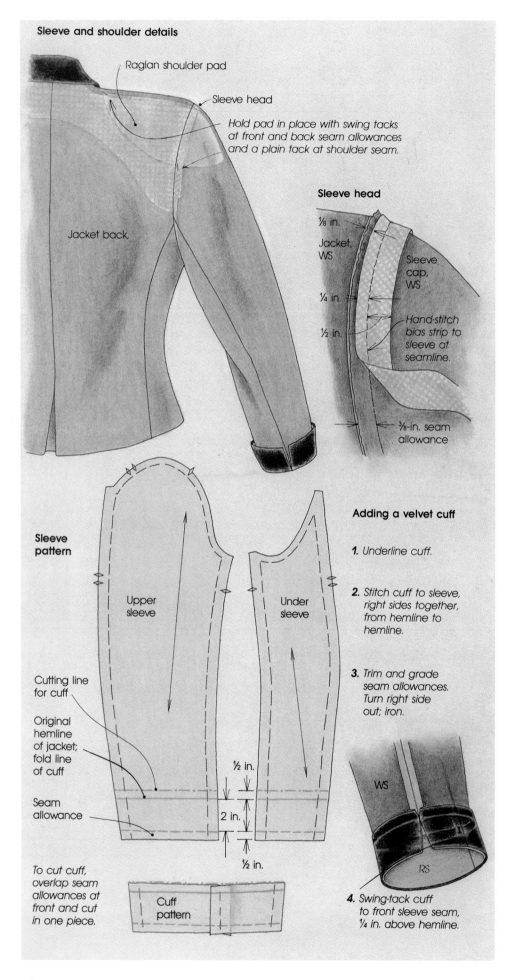

Sleeve and shoulder details

Raglan shoulder pad

Sleeve head

Hold pad in place with swing tacks at front and back seam allowances and a plain tack at shoulder seam.

Jacket back.

Sleeve head

1/8 in.

Jacket, WS

Sleeve cap, WS

1/4 in.

1/2 in.

Hand-stitch bias strip to sleeve at seamline.

3/8-in. seam allowance

Sleeve pattern

Upper sleeve

Under sleeve

Cutting line for cuff

Original hemline of jacket; fold line of cuff

Seam allowance

1/2 in.

2 in.

1/2 in.

To cut cuff, overlap seam allowances at front and cut in one piece.

Cuff pattern

Adding a velvet cuff

1. Underline cuff.

2. Stitch cuff to sleeve, right sides together, from hemline to hemline.

3. Trim and grade seam allowances. Turn right side out; iron.

WS

RS

4. Swing-tack cuff to front sleeve seam, 1/4 in. above hemline.

to the hem. Match one edge of the wigan, which is 1/4 in. wider than the hem allowance, to the raw edge of the hem and attach it with straight machine stitching (drawing, p. 15). Blind-catchstitch the hem in place, down the center of the hem. (This is faster than the custom-tailoring method of catchstitching and hand-basting a bias strip to the jacket body, with the extra 1/4 in. extending above the hem's raw edge.) When the hem is folded in place, the extra 1/4 in. lies next to the jacket body (in custom jackets it lies next to the hem allowance). This placement is fine as long as the fabric has enough body so that the extra width doesn't show on the right side of the jacket, as it would with lighter fabrics.

The box pleat on the Dior jacket requires two pieces of wigan; each piece breaks at the center back and isn't included in the hem of the pleat underlay. If your jacket has no pleat, you can use a continuous bias strip or a separate piece for each garment section.

The lower two-thirds of the armscye is taped with a 1/4-in.-wide plain-weave cotton tape. The tape can be used to ease the back of the armscye to cup the fabric around the curved shape of the back arm, ensuring that the sleeve and jacket hang better. It also prevents stretching of the armscye when the sleeve is set and when the jacket is worn.

Plain-weave tape isn't usually available to the home sewer, but I prefer plain weave rather than heavier twill tape. I save the selvages from silk organza and silk blouse fabric for this purpose. Apply the tape just inside the seamline in the seam allowance, beginning on the jacket front about 3 in. below the shoulder seam, continuing under the arm, and ending on the back about

The jacket's flared peplum may look as though it has a functional box pleat, but this is the limit of its spread.

4 in. from the shoulder seam. Simply straight-stitch down the tape's middle.

Close to the vest

Designed to be worn as a blouse, the unlined vest repeats the princess line of the jacket and has the same jet buttons in a smaller size. Fusible knit interfacing is used for the neckline and armhole facings. They're understitched by machine and hand-tacked at the seamlines so they won't roll out at the edges. The vest has slightly extended shoulders kept firm with small shoulder pads that are merely 6½-in.-dia. circles of bonded fiberfill folded slightly off-center. The pads are secured at the neckpoints and armscyes with ½-in.-long swing tacks.

Tricks up the sleeve

The high cap sleeves of the jacket are smoothly set into the armholes; there's no seam rippling or dimpling across the cap. One useful industrial technique for setting the sleeve smoothly is to use only ⅜-in.-wide seam allowances around the armhole and sleeve, which is less difficult to ease than the typical ⅝ in. that home sewers use.

Another trick is to apply a narrow bias-cut sleeve head, which was done in the Dior jacket. I even use a sleeve head in blouses to eliminate dimples across the cap and to serve as a buffer between the seam allowances and the sleeve. Apply the sleeve head after setting the sleeve and before putting in the shoulder pads (drawing at top right, facing page). Cut a wigan strip ¾ in. wide and 13 in. long, and position the edge of the sleeve head on the wrong side of the sleeve about ⅛ in. from the raw edge. Hand-stitch it with a running stitch on the seamline. A ¼-in. width of the strip overlaps the seam allowance, while ½ in. extends into the sleeve cap. In the Dior jacket, the sleeve head is set slightly off-center with 7 in. toward the front and 6 in. toward the back.

At first glance, the rounded shoulder line of the Dior jacket appears to have less padding than we've seen in recent years; it's an illusion created by the thick, raglan shoulder pads that extend well into the sleeves. These pads support the sleeve caps so they can't collapse. The shoulder pads are tacked lightly at the neckpoint and sewn to the front and back armscye seam allowances with short swing tacks (drawing at top left, facing page). The swing tacks hold the pads in position but still allow them to float without distorting the lines of the jacket.

The 2-in.-wide turned-up velvet cuffs look wonderful and are easy to add to jacket sleeves (bottom drawing and photo, facing page). On the Dior jacket, the two-piece sleeve was cut 2½ in. longer than the finished sleeve length so it would fold back to make a cuff; the same pattern was used to cut the velvet, but with ½ in. added above the wrist for attachment to the lining and for the turn. The rectangular-shaped cuffs flare when turned back. If the sleeve pattern of your jacket narrows toward the wrist, flare the facing and cuff to match the flare of the sleeve; otherwise, the cuff edge will be smaller than the sleeve and won't turn outward as it should.

Bagging the smooth lining

The Dior jacket lining has a ½-in.-deep pleat at the center back that tapers to nothing just below the waistline (photo at right, p. 18). Since the back jacket pleat is only decorative, the lining covers it completely. All the lining pieces are cut to fit the *inside* of the jacket perfectly; the lining's shoulders have a greater slant than the jacket's shoulders, and the lining's sleeve caps are shallower (drawing below). When applying this idea, you'll have to experiment, as shoulder pads vary in thickness; just remember that the angle of the shoulder seam must increase with the thickness of the pad.

At the underarm, the linings for the side panel and undersleeve are cut higher than the jacket and extend into the armscye. The higher cut clears the jacket's armscye seam allowances, which stands up under the arm and ensures a more attractive sleeve.

Bagging is one of the easiest industrial techniques to learn. Instead of attaching just the front facings and neckline of the lining to the jacket by machine, and the sleeves and hem by hand, you apply the lining almost entirely by machine (drawing sequence, p. 18). The trick is to pull the final seam, the jacket's hem, through a slit left open in the center-back lining. To make the bagging concept clear, I'll explain how to bag the lining for a jacket without a pleat.

Before applying the lining, complete the jacket shell, sew the velvet cuffs to the sleeve extensions, and sew the collar and facings to the jacket. In custom tailoring, the undercollar is attached to the upper collar, and the facing is attached to the lapel before the neckline seams—upper collar to facing, undercollar to jacket—are stitched. I was impressed because this had been done in the Dior jacket so that the four seams meet precisely at the notch.

Press the jacket hem in place and trim it to a scant 1½ in. Turn the jacket wrong side out.

Before cutting the lining, correct the pattern so that the lining will fit the inside of the jacket smoothly. Then assemble the lining body and set the sleeves, but leave a 10-in.-long opening in the upper part of the back seam; press.

With right sides together, pin the edges of the lining and jacket facings and necklines together, matching the notches and shoulder seams (drawing at left, p. 18). Stitch, beginning and ending even with the raw edge of the jacket hemline. Press the seam toward the lining and catchstitch the edges of the front jacket facings to the jacket underlining. At the shoulder, sew the facing/lining seam to the shoulder pad. Turn the jacket right side out.

Straighten the jacket, turn the cuffs up, and insert the sleeve linings into the sleeves. Check that the sleeve linings aren't twisted and that the seamlines of the jacket and lining match. At the wrist, fold the raw edge of the lining under and pin it in place

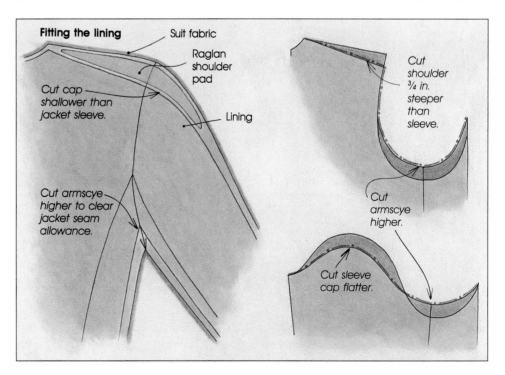

Fitting the lining — Suit fabric — Raglan shoulder pad — Lining

Cut cap shallower than jacket sleeve.

Cut armscye higher to clear jacket seam allowance.

Cut shoulder ¾ in. steeper than sleeve.

Cut armscye higher.

Cut sleeve cap flatter.

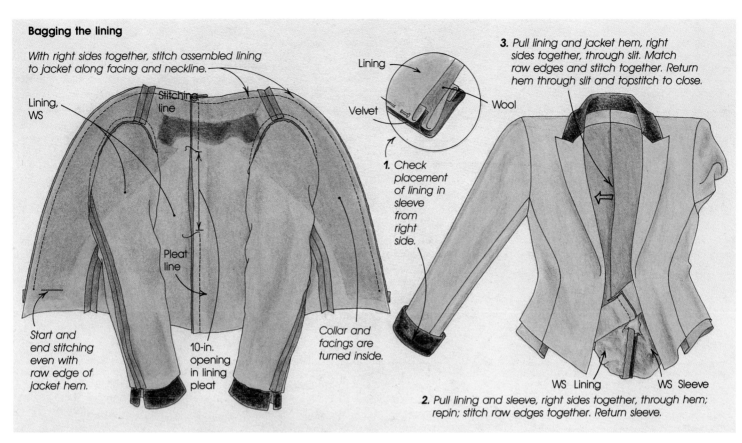

Bagging the lining

With right sides together, stitch assembled lining to jacket along facing and neckline.

Lining, WS

Stitching line

Pleat line

Start and end stitching even with raw edge of jacket hem.

10-in. opening in lining pleat

Collar and facings are turned inside.

Lining

Velvet

Wool

1. Check placement of lining in sleeve from right side.

2. Pull lining and sleeve, right sides together, through hem; repin; stitch raw edges together. Return sleeve.

WS Lining

WS Sleeve

3. Pull lining and jacket hem, right sides together, through slit. Match raw edges and stitch together. Return hem through slit and topstitch to close.

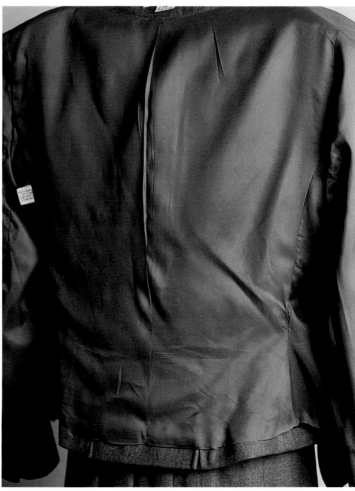

The bagged lining is almost entirely inserted with machine stitching. It has only a tiny fold at the hem (left). The lining has a pleat for wearing ease only above the waist; since the jacket pleat doesn't open, the lining fits like a glove in the peplum area (right).

to the seam allowance of the velvet cuff so the lining fold is above the wrist (detail in drawing at top right, facing page).

Reach into the jacket through the open hem and pull out the sleeves; repin the cuff and lining from the wrong side with right sides together; I fold the lining under ⅝ in., but I stitch only a ⅜-in. seam so there's a small pleat in the lining at the wrist. Stitch, and then tack the cuff/facing seam to the sleeve seams with short swing tacks so the cuff won't shift. Replace the sleeves right sides out.

Check the lining length; it should extend ½ in. to ¾ in. below the pressed hemline of the jacket. Hand-tack the seam allowances of the lining and jacket at the shoulder point and at the jacket underarm to anchor the lining so that it won't billow away from the jacket shell.

Reach through the center-back lining slit and pull out the lining and jacket hems. With right sides together, match and pin the raw edges of the jacket and lining hems together, and stitch from facing to facing.

Straighten the jacket; then machine-stitch the raw lining edges at center back together as much as possible. Use a slipstitch to finish the remaining 2 in. to 3 in. by hand. Also finish the hem by hand-stitching the lining fold down at the corners.

A skirt with flair

The Dior skirt was commercially pleated after the right-side seam and hem were completed. Many large cities have pleaters who will double-pleat your fabric for about $35 and up (one mail-order source is Koppel Pleating, 890 Garrison Ave., Bronx, NY 10474; 212-893-1500). When sending fabric out to pleaters, give them your hip and waist measurements; they'll taper the pleats for you from hip to waist.

The pleats in the Dior skirt are stitched closed on the wrong side above the hip, so the stitching doesn't show. The left-side seam was stitched through all layers from the hem to the bottom of the zipper opening; then the zipper was inserted. The waistband application was standard and finished with the stitching-in-the-ditch technique.

If you don't want to have your fabric professionally pleated, you can set the pleats yourself. The secret to making double pleats that lie flat is to stagger the folds so they don't coincide. I'll use the measurements from the Dior suit to explain this.

To make double 1-in.-wide pleats (drawing at right), you start with a pleat allowance that's 4 in. wide. Mark the position of the pleat lines—the ones that meet on the right side of the skirt—4 in. apart with thread or chalk. On the Dior skirt, the lines are on the lengthwise grain from hip to hem. Match the pairs of lines and baste

them together. With the right side up, fold the pleat underlay to the left. Cover the fabric with a damp press cloth and press only the basted line from 7 in. below the waist (hipline) to the hem; don't press the fold on the underside or above the hipline.

Turn the fabric over and taper the pleats to fit the body from hipline to waist. Subtract the waist measurement from the hip measurement and divide the difference by the number of pleats. For example, the Dior skirt is 27¾ in. at the waist and 42½ in. at the hip. The difference, 14¾ in., when divided by the number of pleats (18) is 0.82 in. Since this fraction is hard to work with, I'd pin-baste an extra ¾ in. (0.75 in.) into each pleat underlay (⅜ in. in each fabric layer) at the waist. This doesn't make the waist small enough, so I'd increase a few pleats another ¼ in. All the pleats don't have to be the same size. Baste from the pin to the previous basting at the hipline to form small darts around the abdomen.

Now make the double pleats. Refold each pleat as shown to make two smaller pleats, but make the pleat nearer the garment ⅛ in. wider than the inside pleat. The folds are staggered, which reduces the bulk; the folds on the underside are less likely to show on the right side. Straighten and smooth each double pleat; press. Machine-stitch along the basting for 7 in. below the waistline, pivot, and stitch for ¼ in. to secure the double pleat; backstitch. □

Claire B. Shaeffer shared details of how to make a Chanel jacket in Threads, *No. 23, p. 24. Her latest book,* Claire Shaeffer's Fabric Sewing Guide *(Chilton, 1989) was reviewed in issue 25, p. 12.*

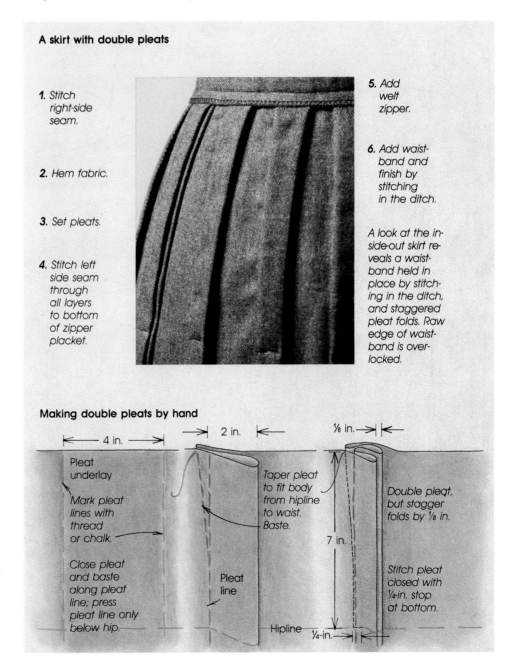

A skirt with double pleats

1. Stitch right-side seam.

2. Hem fabric.

3. Set pleats.

4. Stitch left side seam through all layers to bottom of zipper placket.

5. Add welt zipper.

6. Add waistband and finish by stitching in the ditch.

A look at the inside-out skirt reveals a waistband held in place by stitching in the ditch, and staggered pleat folds. Raw edge of waistband is overlocked.

Making double pleats by hand

|← 4 in. →| |← 2 in. →| |⅛ in.→|←|

Pleat underlay

Mark pleat lines with thread or chalk.

Close pleat and baste along pleat line; press pleat line only below hip.

Pleat line

Taper pleat to fit body from hipline to waist. Baste.

7 in.

Hipline ¼-in.

Double pleat, but stagger folds by ⅛ in.

Stitch pleat closed with ¼-in. stop at bottom.

Fabulous Welt Pockets

How to make a two-way coat pocket

by David Page Coffin

among my favorite pockets is the single-welt side pocket that I found on a London Fog raincoat, years before I even considered sewing clothes for myself. Cleverly concealed just inside the opening was another opening that led to the inside of the coat. It was subtle; you didn't slip into it inadvertantly. But once I noticed, it was obvious that the opening was there so that I could reach through to my pants pockets without unbuttoning the raincoat. I was delighted; surely this was one of the unmentioned perks of adult life, reserved for

those with the good judgement to wear a London Fog!

Once I discovered that I was a sewer, I began to understand why I liked pockets. They're the part of a garment that I get the most use from, and their construction is among the most satisfying steps in the making of any article of clothing. So when I finally felt the need to make my own raincoat (see Threads #19), I naturally undertook to decipher that intriguing two-way welt-covered opening. What follows on pp. 22 and 23 is the step-by-step method for making your own. It's a great pocket for

any knee-length topcoat. If the pocket sounds good, but you think that perfect welts are beyond you, take a look at the techniques on the facing page; I think you'll change your mind. ⇨

David Page Coffin is an associate editor of Threads.

The perfect welt is the entrance to the perfect pocket: a double entry trick that lets you get into your pants or skirt pocket without unbuttoning your coat. Here's a step-by-step guide to making both the pocket and the welt.

From *Threads* magazine (December 1990) 32:54-57

Perfecting the welt

by Shermane Fouché

You could hardly ask for a more basic garment detail than a pocket welt. Welts are nothing more than faced shapes. But unless they're perfect (points sharp, edges straight, and facings neatly out of sight on every side), welts are just sore thumbs: hard-to-miss little proclamations of inadequate sewing skills. Having recently made a lot of welts in wool gabardine, like the one at left, I have come up with some techniques that virtually guarantee success. They apply equally well to other similar fabrics and to any faced shape, even to collar points.

Cutting out—Cut both the welt and a lining from the welt pattern, which should include ⅝-in. seam allowances. You'll trim all the seams later, but the wide allowances make it easy to press the seams open fully, especially in a wiry fabric like gabardine. I always use a natural fiber lining, usually silk crepe or broadcloth, instead of rayon, because it handles so much more easily. Cut out a fusible interfacing (I like Armo-Weft or Easy-Knit) for the gab, with the grain parallel to the welt opening edge. Trim its allowances to ¼ in. before fusing.

Drawing precise seamlines—Lay the lining and the fused gab pieces wrong sides together, interfacing up. Trimming with rotary cutter and straight edge will assure all edges are true. Then, with chalk and a see-through ruler, draw the seamlines of the welt shape on the interfacing.

This welt is asymmetrical, with one broad point and one narrow point. Any point that's less than a right angle has a tendency to push out too far, so I correct the seamlines by moving the point ⅛ to ¼ in. in from the actual corner, depending on the weight of the fabric, and curving the ½ in. of seamline on either side in to meet the new point, as shown in the drawing at top right.

Favoring the lining—Pin the lining to the gab with a row of pins down the center of the welt, lengthwise. To make sure that the lining doesn't show on the finished welt, make the lining a little smaller by "favoring" it, which means shifting its raw edge slightly away from the gab's edge, as you can see

in the drawing at center right. With the lining side up, slide your left hand fingers under the welt and bend the edges toward your thumb, which slides the lining edge about 1/16 in. beyond the edge of the gab. Work along each edge, pinning the favoring in place.

When the whole welt is pinned, carefully baste along the exact seamline including the corrected point. Remove the pins and machine-sew the welt just inside the basting. Sew the ½ in. on either side of each point with tiny stitches (about 25 per inch) and stitch across the point with two or three stitches.

Pressing, trimming, and turning—Press the welt as sewn, then press the seams fully open over an edge board, or point presser (see *Basics*, No. 32, p. 8). Now trim the seams so the lining is ⅛ in., the gab is ¼ in., and each point is within a few threads of the edge.

The more thorough your edge pressing, the more easily the welt will turn; I use an ordinary point turner for the points. Before pressing the turned welt, baste the sewn edges as you roll the facing out of sight. Sometimes a little blister of fullness forms at the narrow point; with careful basting this will be held in place and won't be seen after the welt is topstitched and stitched down.

Before giving the welt its final press, I like to wrap a metal ruler with a single layer of muslin and lay it next to the long welt edge, pressing the welt against it to create a perfectly straight edge, as shown in the drawing at bottom right. I cover both with another press cloth and steam press, then press with a wooden clapper. I repeat this for the shorter edge so the point is as straight as possible.

Finishing—Even with all these efforts, sometimes one edge is straighter than another. Try to perfect the long open edge first, and topstitch it as close to the edge as possible. You can make subtle corrections to the shorter edge as you stitch it into place.

Shermane Fouché is a custom designer in San Francisco who teaches classes in sewing and design at the Sewing Workshop and across the country.

Correcting seamlines at a narrow point

¼ to ⅛ in.
½ in.
Gabardine
½ in.
Corrected point
Lining
Interfacing

Favoring the lining

Bend seam allowance toward gab side to offset edges. Pin along seamline.

Steaming edges straight

Press welt against muslin-wrapped ruler.

Cover with press cloth. Press, steam, press with clapper.

Sewing the double-entry pocket

For each pocket, you'll need: a finished, lined welt, approximately 7½ in. long on the raw edge, (see p. 21 for step-by-step instructions); two identical rectangles of pocketing material, approximately 14 in. long by 12½ in. wide; and an 8 in. strip of lining selvage, ½ in. wide.

Key

☐ RS Pocketing piece #1   ☐ WS
☐ RS Pocketing piece #2   ☐ WS
☐ RS Coat front   ☐ WS
☐ Welt   ☐ Welt lining   ☐ Selvage strip

1. Mark pocket opening and welt position on coat front (RS): *Draw line A equal in length to welt, beginning approximately 7 to 8 in. from coat front edge and angling as desired. Draw line B, ½ in. away and ⅜ in. shorter.*

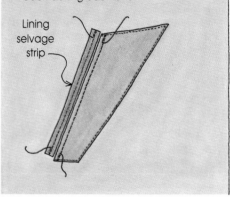

7 to 8 in.

A

B

½ in.

⅜ in.

Coat front edge

2. Attach welt and selvage lining strip to coat front: *Position welt RS down with seamline (¼ in. seam allowance) on line A. Stitch, backtacking each end. Center selvage lining on line B, selvage away from welt, and stitch, backtacking each end.*

Lining selvage strip

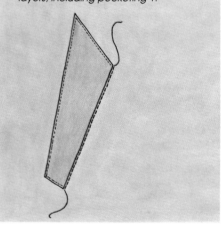

5. Slash pocketing: *¼ in. from welt seamline, slash pocketing only, angling ends.*

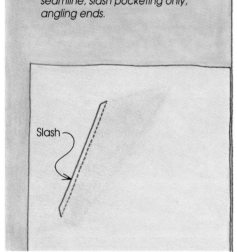

Slash

6. Turn pocket to wrong side: *Push pocket and welt seam allowance through coat slash. On inside, turn pocketing through its own slash.*

7. Topstitch welt to secure: *On RS of coat front, smooth layers, press, and stitch just below welt seam, through all layers, including pocketing 1.*

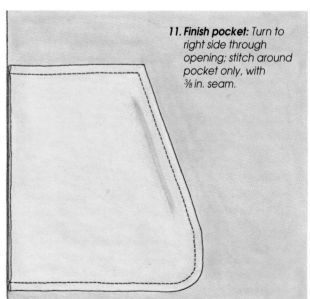

10. Attach pocketing 2: *Position pocketing 2 under pocketing 1, WSs together, sandwiching coat front between them. Stitch with ¼ in. seam around 3 sides, in pocket shape. Trim.*

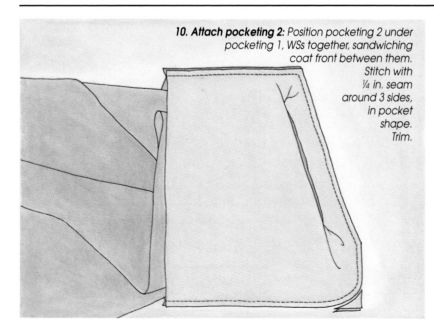

11. Finish pocket: *Turn to right side through opening; stitch around pocket only, with ⅜ in. seam.*

3. Attach pocketing 1: *Position RS down, flush with coat front edge, and 1½ in. above welt. Turn coat to WS to stitch, along previous seam on line A, backtacking ends.*

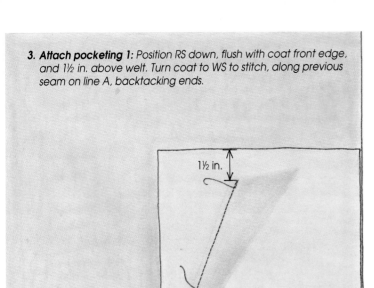

1½ in.

4. Slash coat: *Turn coat front to RS. Lift pocketing and welt seam allowance; slash exactly between lines A and B, angling the cut to meet endpoints top and bottom.*

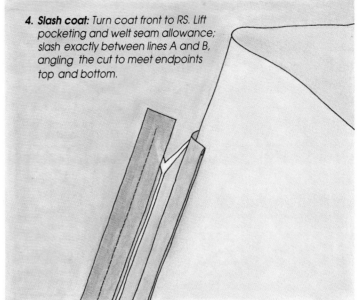

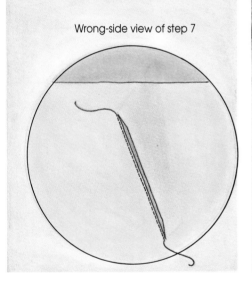

Wrong-side view of step 7

8. Finish raw edge of coat slash: *Turn lining strip to inside and topstitch (on WS of coat).*

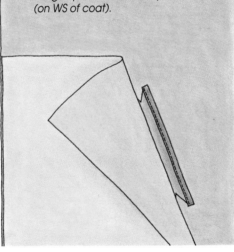

9. Introduce pocketing 2: *With pocketing 1 smooth and flat, position pocketing 2 on top, RS down and trim both 1½ in. above slash.*

1½ in.

12. Finish raw edge of pocketing slash: *Turn coat to RS and fold out of way. Zigzag raw edge of pocketing 1 to pocketing 2, or turn it under and topstitch.*

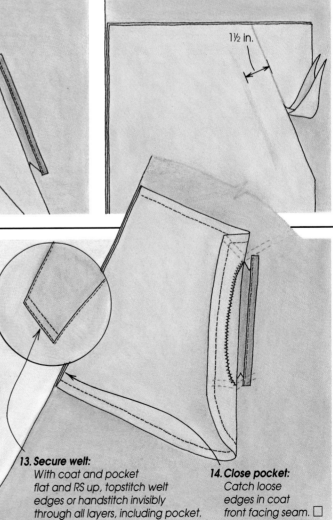

13. Secure welt: *With coat and pocket flat and RS up, topstitch welt edges or handstitch invisibly through all layers, including pocket.*

14. Close pocket: *Catch loose edges in coat front facing seam.* □

Illustrations by Phoebe Gaughan

Vent First

Simplify construction of a classic two-piece jacket sleeve

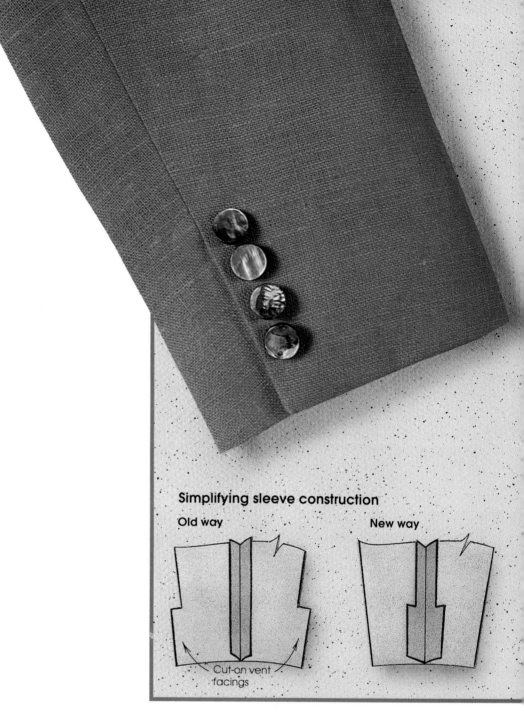

Simplifying sleeve construction

Old way

New way

Cut-on vent facings

by Shirley McKeown

the traditional method of making two-piece jacket sleeves is to complete them (after confirming the fit, usually with a muslin) by finishing the seams, vents, hems, and sometimes even the linings, before they're attached. This saves wear, avoids wrinkling of the jacket during construction, and makes the process easier as well, by allowing you to do as much as possible while the sleeve is flat—while only one of the two seams is finished. (If your pattern doesn't have two-piece sleeves, see "Drafting a two-piece sleeve" on pp. 26-27.)

For some reason, tailoring methods have always advocated sewing the seam that doesn't include the vent first, as in

the drawing above. I've discovered that if you start with the vent seam instead, the job becomes easier still, because you don't have to finish the vent within the small opening of the closed sleeve. The process I use is shown in full on the facing page. Here's a brief rundown of the steps involved:

Constructing the sleeve

To prepare the sleeve pieces, first make sure when you cut them out that both vent openings have cut-on facings, as in the drawings shown here. If your pattern doesn't have them, they can be added easily. Typical ones are shown in the last drawing on p. 27. Press the hems in place on all four pieces; I use a hem gauge, like

Dritz's Ezy-Hem. Next, staystitch the hem and vent edges at ¼ in., and the underarm at ½ in. on the undersleeve section. If you're using an underlining, apply the sleeve underlining pieces to the wrong side of the sleeve pieces before staystitching, then press.

I stitch the seam with the vent from top to bottom, switching to my maximum stitch size at the dot that marks the start of the vent, to baste the vent closed. I clip the vent facing on the undersleeve so I can fold the facing over to form the underlap, then finish both vent corners, forming the hem. I like to miter the overlap corner so there is no seamline at the edge (see *Tips*, No. 38, p. 20), but I seam the underlap corner. A bias

From *Threads* magazine (December 1991) 38:36-39

Two-piece sleeve construction steps

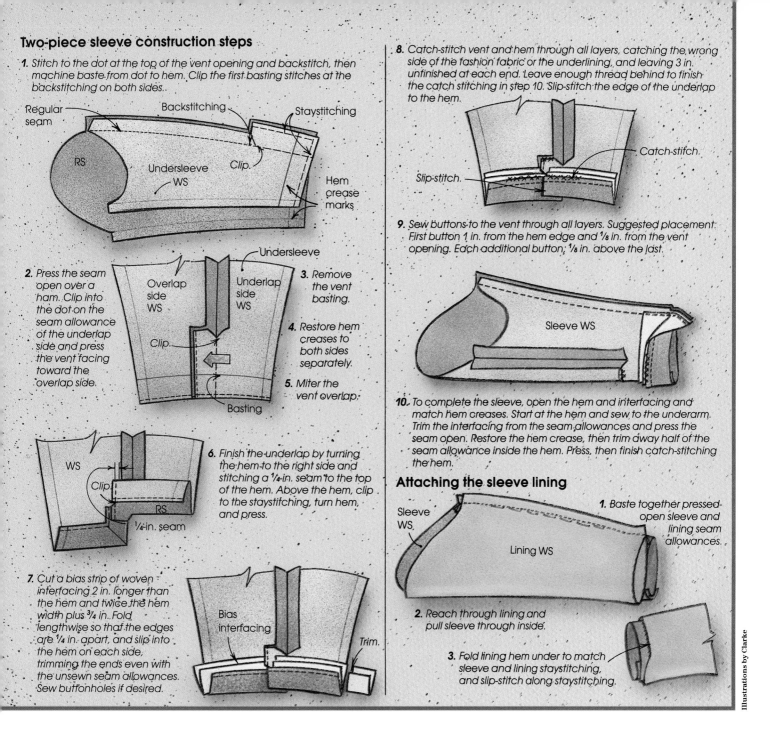

1. Stitch to the dot at the top of the vent opening and backstitch, then machine baste from dot to hem. Clip the first basting stitches at the backstitching on both sides.

Regular seam · Backstitching · Staystitching · RS · Undersleeve WS · Clip. · Hem crease marks

2. Press the seam open over a ham. Clip into the dot on the seam allowance of the underlap side and press the vent facing toward the overlap side.

Overlap side WS · Undersleeve · Underlap side WS · Clip. · Basting

3. Remove the vent basting.

4. Restore hem creases to both sides separately.

5. Miter the vent overlap.

WS · Clip. · RS · ¼-in. seam

6. Finish the underlap by turning the hem to the right side and stitching a ¼-in. seam to the top of the hem. Above the hem, clip to the staystitching, turn hem, and press.

7. Cut a bias strip of woven interfacing 2 in. longer than the hem and twice the hem width plus ¾ in. Fold lengthwise so that the edges are ¼ in. apart, and slip into the hem on each side, trimming the ends even with the unsewn seam allowances. Sew buttonholes if desired.

Bias interfacing · Trim.

8. Catch-stitch vent and hem through all layers, catching the wrong side of the fashion fabric or the underlining, and leaving 3 in. unfinished at each end. Leave enough thread behind to finish the catch stitching in step 10. Slip-stitch the edge of the underlap to the hem.

Slip-stitch. · Catch-stitch.

9. Sew buttons to the vent through all layers. Suggested placement: First button 1 in. from the hem edge and ⅛ in. from the vent opening. Each additional button, ⅛ in. above the last.

Sleeve WS

10. To complete the sleeve, open the hem and interfacing and match hem creases. Start at the hem and sew to the underarm. Trim the interfacing from the seam allowances and press the seam open. Restore the hem crease, then trim away half of the seam allowance inside the hem. Press, then finish catch-stitching the hem.

Attaching the sleeve lining

Sleeve WS · Lining WS

1. Baste together pressed-open sleeve and lining seam allowances.

2. Reach through lining and pull sleeve through inside.

3. Fold lining hem under to match sleeve and lining staystitching, and slip-stitch along staystitching.

Illustrations by Clarke

---

fold of compatible woven interfacing, called a hem roll, fits easily into the pressed sleeve hem and, with the use of a hem gauge and steam iron, can be made to take whatever curve the jacket sleeve hem may have. The edges of the two layers of interfacing and the hem are graded to keep the hem from showing on the right side of the sleeve.

At this point I catch-stitch all layers to the outer fabric. I sew on the buttons, and the vent is complete. Next I stitch the remaining seam, and finally make and attach the lining, as described below.

This method is a perfect example of the concept of unit construction, in which all the parts of one section of a garment are completed before attaching it to or adding another section. When organized like this, a pleasant task becomes an enjoyable one.

Adding the lining

Prepare the sleeve lining (cut 1 in. shorter than sleeve) by staystitching the hem at ¼ in. and the sleeve cap at ½ in., then stitch both seams. With finished sleeve and sleeve lining wrong sides out, place the corresponding undersleeve and lining together, matching the two seams. Stitch their lengthwise seam allowances together by hand with long, loose running stitches beginning and ending 3 in. from the hem and armhole. Reach through the lining, grab the sleeve vent area, and pull it back through the lining

so the hem is enclosed within the end of the lining, as in the last drawing above.

Attach the lining hem to the sleeve hem by folding under the ¼-in. staystitching line on the lining hem and pinning it to the staystitching line of the fashion fabric hem. The extra lining fabric will create the 'drop' in the lining at the sleeve hem. Slip-stitch the lining to the sleeve hem all around.

Turn the sleeve right side out, and the lining should drop into place. The sleeve is now completely finished and ready to attach to the jacket. □

Shirley McKeown has taught clothing construction at G Street Fabrics in Maryland for the past 10 years. ⇨

Drafting a two-piece jacket sleeve from a one-piece pattern

by Margaret Komives

It's well known that two-piece sleeves have a much better shape than one-piece sleeves. The extra seam is an added shaping opportunity for the patternmaker, and also offers the tailor twice as many seams to adjust for a better fit. In my tailoring classes I recommend that students start with patterns that feature two-piece sleeves. But all too often they arrive with a one-piece sleeve pattern—either because they liked everything else about the pattern, or because they just didn't notice.

Whatever the reason, if you've got a one-piece sleeve pattern, with a little patience and some judgement you can draft a two-piece pattern from it. It is not an exact technique by any means and personal preference enters in, but the results I've gotten with the following methods have been very satisfactory.

Why not just use the sleeve pattern from another jacket? Unfortunately, that would require using the armscye from the other pattern, too, and transferring the armscye (which usually involves three body pieces) is a far more tricky job than redrawing the sleeve.

There are two types of one-piece sleeves. There's the usual centered-underarm sleeve, shown on the facing page, and then there's the sleeve, shown in the drawings at right, that has the seam offset toward the back of the

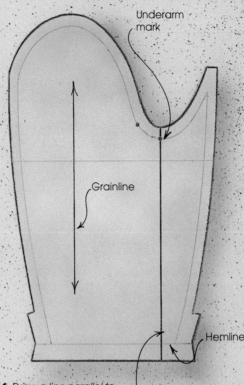

1. Draw a line parallel to the grainline from underarm mark to hem.

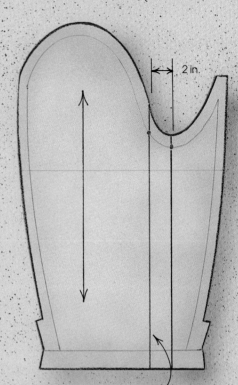

2. Draw a parallel line 2 in. from first line, from armscye to hemline.

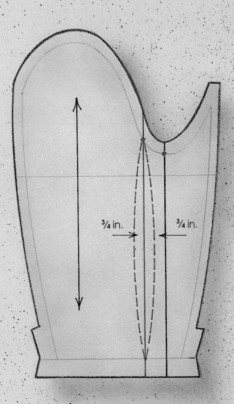

3. Measure ¾ in. to either side of new line at elbow, and connect seam and hem with curves through the new points. Cut on curved lines.

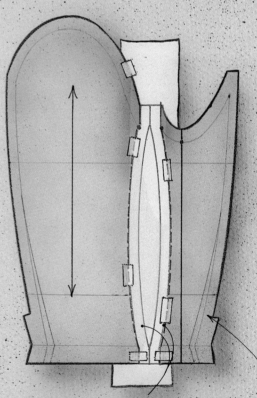

4. Add seam allowances to each side, marking the new seams at hem and armscye. Redraw vent seams to narrow cuff if necessary.

Converting symmetrical sleeves

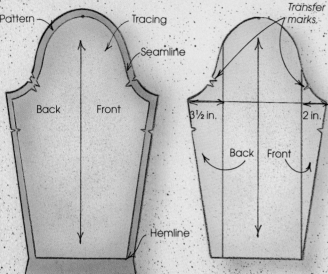

1. Trace original pattern without seam allowances, transferring all markings.

2. On tracing, measure 2 in. in at the end of the front armsyce seam, and 3½ to 4 in. from the back seam. Draw vertical lines parallel to the grain from armscye to hem. Cut tracing apart on these lines; tape pieces together on original seamline, matching notches.

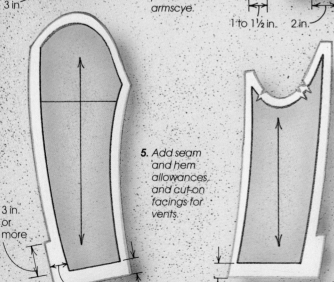

3. Measure ¾ in. in at elbow in front, and in 3 in. at hem in back. Connect armscye to hem through these points. Drop the back seam ⅝ in. for ease if desired.

4. Drop new grainlines from the armscye seam ends to the hemline. Measure out from the front 1 in. to 1½ in. and in from the back 2 in., and connect the new points to the armscye.

5. Add seam and hem allowances, and cut-on facings for vents.

underarm so that when it's sewn, it gives the appearance of a two-piece sleeve and can even have a vent. This type is the easiest to convert so I'll cover it first.

Converting the offset-seam sleeve

Always begin by pressing the pattern. Then draw a line through the underarm mark (which all American-made patterns have) parallel to the grainline and the length of the pattern. Next, draw a line two inches away from and parallel to this line toward the front of the sleeve, from seamline to hemline.

In the elbow area which lies in the center of the section usually marked "Ease" on the pattern, measure and mark ½ in. to ¾ in. away from the second drawn line on each side. Draw identical curved lines from seamline to hemline through the marked points, either with a curved ruler, or following a favorite two-pieced sleeve pattern, or by your own experienced hand. These will be stitching lines, so mark them as such.

Cut the pattern on the curved lines and add a ⅝-in. seam allowance to each. It should be easy to line up these seams later if you're careful to mark the upper and lower ends as in the last drawing on the facing page. That's all there is to it.

Before you move on, check the sleeve width at the hemline. Many jackets come with a sleeve that is much too wide at the wrist. Measure a favorite jacket for reference. I recommend about ten inches for a size 12, six inches on the upper sleeve, four inches on the undersleeve. You can narrow the wrist by redrawing the vent seamlines: Take half the distance (usually about 2 in. overall) off on each side by tapering the seams in gradually from the armscye to the elbow, then taper a little more severely from elbow to wrist.

It's always a good idea to cut a test garment to check for drape, fit, etc. Make sure the vent lies in a good location,

not too far to the front, nor underneath, where those lovely buttons won't show. In a size 12 there should be about two inches from the underarm line to the vent placement line. If the vent falls too far underneath, add to the undersleeve and take off from the upper, keeping a nice curve in the process.

Converting symmetrical sleeves

The symmetrical sleeve with the seam at the underarm, as shown at left, is much more common. The procedure for converting it is slightly more complex, but it's not difficult.

Begin by tracing the pattern without seam allowances. Trace off the stitching lines, darts, grainline, and any other important marks the pattern indicates. If it's a multisize pattern, draw in the stitching lines by measuring ⅝ in. in from the cutting line for your size. Cut the pattern on the stitching lines.

The drawings at left show the procedure. Basically, we're cutting off the side seams and piecing them together to make up an undersleeve pattern piece, then drawing new seams. Occasionally you'll encounter a pattern so narrow at the bottom that the vertical lines you need to make the cuts (see Step 2) hit the existing side seams before reaching the hem. If only one line hits a side seam, don't do anything. If both lines hit, add tissue so you can redraw the side seams wide enough for the vertical lines to reach the hem.

When you draw the back seam on the upper sleeve piece (see Step 3), you can add ⅝ in. to its length to create ease. You can add this length to the pattern in the previous procedure, too, but you'll have to redraw the hemline on the upper sleeve piece. The width of the sleeve at the hemline can also be corrected, as described above.

Margaret Komives is a frequent contributor to Threads.

Contemporary Tailoring

Construct a classic cardigan jacket completely by machine

by Cecelia Podolak

The chic, tailored lines of this jacket don't reveal its secret: modern fusible interfacings replace traditional hand tailoring. The iron takes the place of the needle in applying these garment-shapers, cutting tailoring time drastically. (Photo by Yvonne Taylor)

*i*f you love the look of tailored jackets, but have always considered them too complicated, mysterious, or time-consuming to sew yourself, you're in for a pleasant surprise. Those sharply pressed front edges that don't stretch, hems that don't sag, nicely rounded sleeve caps, and well-set sleeves are achievable. By combining traditional pressing, contemporary sewing methods, and fusible interfacing, you can make a beautiful jacket that rivals the look and detail of high-end ready-to-wear in less time than you imagine (see photo on facing page).

A real time-saver that won't sacrifice quality is the process method of sewing: performing all related tasks, like fusing interfacing, at one time. I'll explain a sewing sequence that may differ from the one in your pattern.

To try out these new methods (the same ones used in designer ready-to-wear), start with a cardigan-style jacket with patch pockets, which will give you quick results in addition to good looks. After the first project, it will be easy to proceed to a more complex jacket.

Style and fabric considerations

Patterns for cardigan jackets are available in a variety of lengths and styles, both single- and double-breasted. The closer the two rows of buttons and the narrower the overlap on a double-breasted style, the more slenderizing the jacket. A single button placed close to the waistline produces a longer line in the upper part of the body, creating an illusion of height. A below-the-hip length is flattering for tall women, while an at-hip version looks good on petites.

Pattern selection—Instead of buying a pattern in your "usual" size, measure the circumference of your *high bust*, across your upper chest at the underarm. Compare your high bust measure with your actual bust, taken at the fullest part of the chest. If your bust is more than 2 in. larger than the high bust, use your high bust measurement as the bust size when choosing your pattern. This will give you a good fit through the shoulder and neck area, and may only require that you let out the underarm seams to fit it across the bust. I know women who have gone down one or two pattern sizes using this method, and the difference in garment fit is remarkable.

Pin fit and revise your pattern (see *Fitting*, No. 37, pp. 8-10) before you make any other changes.

If the pattern has welt pockets, it will be easier to make if you substitute patch pockets. Use a pocket pattern from another jacket, or design your own, choosing rounded or square corners to harmonize with the jacket's front edge. Draw the shape you want on paper, then place your hand over it to make sure the pocket is large enough to be functional. Try the pocket pattern on the jacket during pin fitting to find placement lines, and mark the jacket pattern. For a final pocket pattern, add seam and hem allowances and cut a lining pattern, as shown in the drawings at right.

Wide seam allowances are easier to press and they lie flatter in the garment, so increase the shoulder, center back, and side seam allowances from ⅝ in. to 1 in. This does not apply to sharply curved seams, such as armscyes, nor is it necessary for the front edges.

Fabric choice—Wool is one of the easiest fibers to shape and mold. The first choice of fabric is 100% wool, but if you choose to work with a blend, select one with at least 50% wool. These techniques will also work well on linen or silk.

Softness, firmness, fineness, and resilience combine to produce the *drape* of a fabric. These are vitally important in sewing and wearing a jacket. *Woolens* are made from low-twist yarns and have a soft hand. Woolen tweeds and many coatings are a good choice for a first project. They are easy to press and hide sewing imperfections. (For more on tweeds, see "Stalking the Real Scottish Tweeds," No. 37, pp. 42-43.)

Worsteds, like gabardine and serge, are woven with highly twisted yarns that have been combed to straighten long fibers and remove short ones. This gives worsteds a durable finish and crisp hand. Unfortunately, it also makes them difficult to press, and causes mistakes to show clearly. The fabric can be very unforgiving, which is why I don't recommend it for a first tailoring project.

Many wool fabrics are commercially preshrunk before sale. If you're not certain that your fabric has been, shrink it before cutting. You can shrink the wool by steaming it thoroughly from the wrong side without a press cloth. Lift, move, and lower your iron, rather than sliding it; handle the damp fabric gently to avoid stretching it. Many dry cleaners will steam-shrink wool for a nominal per-yard fee, and their machines deliver steam under pressure, assuring that the wool is completely dampened.

The jacket process

Before you begin sewing, study the pattern instructions. Don't be afraid to substitute new cutting, marking, and sewing

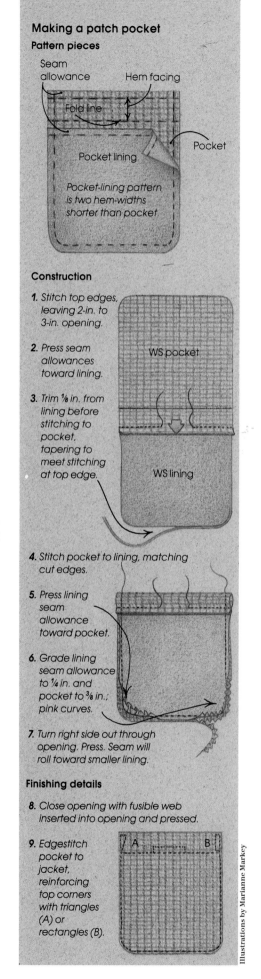

Making a patch pocket
Pattern pieces

Seam allowance
Hem facing
Fold line
Pocket
Pocket lining

Pocket-lining pattern is two hem-widths shorter than pocket.

Construction

1. Stitch top edges, leaving 2-in. to 3-in. opening.

2. Press seam allowances toward lining.

3. Trim ⅛ in. from lining before stitching to pocket, tapering to meet stitching at top edge.

WS pocket

WS lining

4. Stitch pocket to lining, matching cut edges.

5. Press lining seam allowance toward pocket.

6. Grade lining seam allowance to ¼ in. and pocket to ⅜ in.; pink curves.

7. Turn right side out through opening. Press. Seam will roll toward smaller lining.

Finishing details

8. Close opening with fusible web inserted into opening and pressed.

9. Edgestitch pocket to jacket, reinforcing top corners with triangles (A) or rectangles (B).

A   B

Illustrations by Marianne Markey

Cutting and placing the jacket interfacing

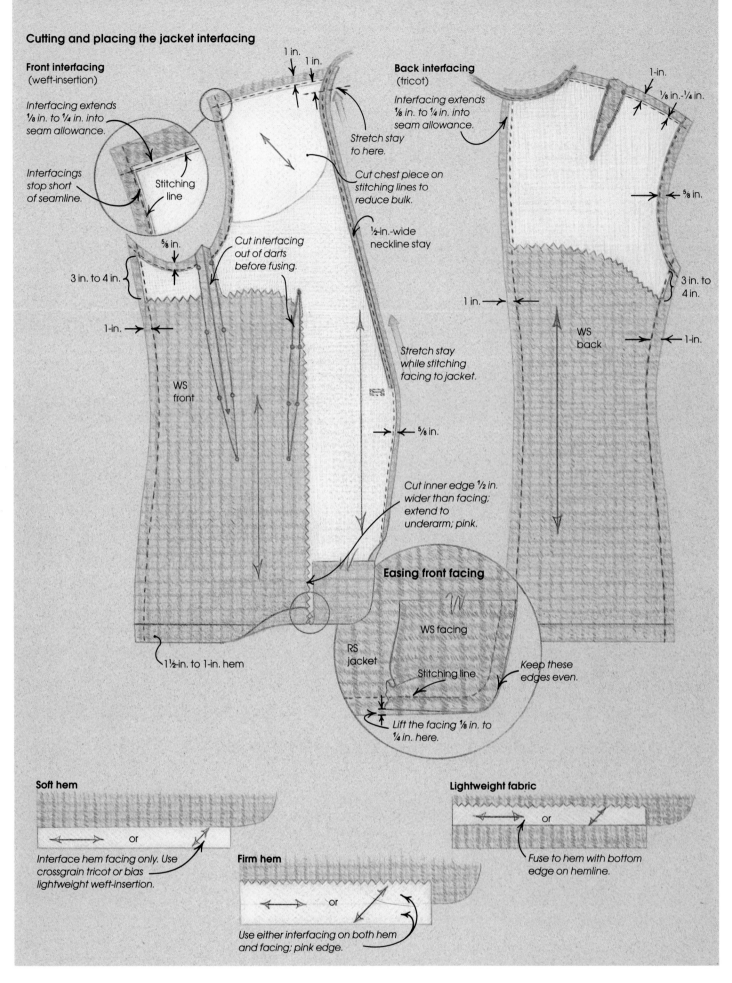

Front interfacing
(weft-insertion)

Interfacing extends ⅛ in. to ¼ in. into seam allowance.

Interfacings stop short of seamline.

Stitching line

⅝ in.

3 in. to 4 in.

1-in.

WS front

1 in. 1 in.

Cut interfacing out of darts before fusing.

Stretch stay to here.

Cut chest piece on stitching lines to reduce bulk.

½-in.-wide neckline stay

Stretch stay while stitching facing to jacket.

⅝ in.

Cut inner edge ½ in. wider than facing; extend to underarm; pink.

1½-in. to 1-in. hem

Back interfacing
(tricot)

Interfacing extends ⅛ in. to ¼ in. into seam allowance.

1-in.

⅛ in.-¼ in.

⅝ in.

3 in. to 4 in.

1 in.

WS back

1-in.

Easing front facing

WS facing

RS jacket

Stitching line

Keep these edges even.

Lift the facing ⅛ in. to ¼ in. here.

Soft hem

or

Interface hem facing only. Use crossgrain tricot or bias lightweight weft-insertion.

Firm hem

or

Use either interfacing on both hem and facing; pink edge.

Lightweight fabric

or

Fuse to hem with bottom edge on hemline.

methods directly on your guide sheet if only traditional tailoring techniques are given. Use a red pencil to show where and how your construction sequence will differ from the pattern's. Convert hand stitching to fusing or machine stitching where possible.

Sewing reference books, such as those listed on p. 33, can be used in the same way you use a cookbook: just as you don't use every recipe, you need only select those sewing techniques that work best for you. Experiment with new ideas, seams, finishes, topstitching, and edge-stitching before working on your garment so you don't get unexpected results. Use scraps of your fashion and lining fabrics to try all the stitching techniques you intend to use.

If your fabric ravels easily, finish the edges of the garment pieces before handling them. If you have a serger, you can serge these edges, but a zigzag stitch will stabilize them as well. If the fabric doesn't need overall finishing, serge or zigzag the lower 2 in. to 3 in. of the front facing that overlaps the hem facing.

Cutting and fusing—Cut out all fabrics—fashion, lining and interfacing—before beginning construction. Cut the fashion fabric and lining according to your pattern, including all the changes you made during pin fitting. Before cutting each piece, pin the pattern tissue to the fabric at each end of the grainline marking and place pattern weights on the edges. I use a rotary cutter with a cutting mat, and a ruler as a guide on straight lines.

To add support to the front and back of your jacket, you will need to interface with fusible interfacing. For more information about kinds and uses of interfacing, see "Fusible interfacings" on p. 32. If your pattern doesn't include instructions or patterns for cutting interfacing pieces, cut them as shown in the drawing on the facing page. I cut the front from weft-insertion interfacing, on the lengthwise grain, following the shape of the front facing and curving outward toward the underarm. The drawing shows where and how much the interfacing extends into the seam allowances.

An extra chest piece fills the hollow of the shoulder. Cut this piece on the bias from tricot or lightweight weft-insertion interfacing, but cut on the stitching lines at shoulder and armscye.

Cut the back interfacing from the lengthwise grain of tricot or lightweight weft-insertion, following the shape and seam allowances shown in the right-hand drawing, facing page. The curve of the bottom of the interfacing lets the fab-

ric hang gracefully in the finished jacket.

Except when they'll be caught in a seam, trim interfacing edges with pinking shears before fusing, to prevent a line from showing through.

You can cut the front facing and, if your pattern has one, the back neck facing according to the pattern pieces. Since you're interfacing the jacket fronts and back, though, you can use a lighter interfacing—tricot or lightweight weft-insertion—for these pieces. Cut a ½-in.-wide stay from weft-insertion interfacing long enough to reach from button to buttonhole around the neck edge.

The sleeve and jacket-bottom hems should always be interfaced, but they move differently from the fronts and back of the jacket and need more flexibility in their interfacing. I use either bias-cut weft-insertion or cross-grain tricot for hems so they will have some "give."

Depending on the crispness of the finished look you want, there are three ways to interface the hems, shown at the bottom of the facing page. For a soft hem, cut interfacing the width of the hem and fuse it only to the hem facing. For a firmer hem, cut twice the width of the hem plus ½ in. Fuse it to both the jacket body and hem facing, pinking the upper edge to avoid a line from pressing. To support a lightweight or soft fabric without making the hem too structured, cut interfacing the width of the hem plus ½ in., pink the upper edge, and fuse it only to the jacket or sleeve (not the facing), aligning one edge to the hemline.

Interface the patch pockets with the same type and weight interfacing you used for the jacket fronts. Cut it on the lengthwise grain to provide the best support for the pocket.

Fuse the interfacing to all the garment pieces, using the directions on p. 32 or the manufacturer's instructions. Before fusing the jacket front and back interfacing, cut away the interfacing along the dart stitching lines.

Sewing the jacket—Stitch the darts and press the folded edges sharp and flat on a cheese block (see *Basics*, No. 37, p. 14) using a clapper to force out the steam and dry the fabric. Press the back-neck darts toward the center back and the darts that shape the waist toward center front. Deep waist darts may need to be clipped in the center so that they will press flat. If your pattern suggests it, slash the center fold and press any large darts open.

Place the pockets on the front sections as indicated on your pattern or determined during the pin fitting. Edgestitch

them in place and add a line of topstitching ¼ in. from the edge if you like.

Sew the center-back, shoulder, side, and sleeve seams. Press these seams open, using a clapper to flatten them. When underpressing (from the wrong side), dampen the fabric with a dauber and iron directly on the fabric. Top-pressing (from the right side of the garment) always needs a press cloth between the fabric and the iron. Lift, move, and lower the iron, rather than sliding it; let the fabric cool and dry before moving it. (For more information about pressing, see the article on pp. 34-37). Stay-stitch the neck edge for ease in setting the facings.

Sew the shoulder seams of the front and back facings, and press them open. Pin the facings to the front edges of the jacket with the jacket on top. The front facing sometimes puts stress on the jacket front, causing a "pulled" look at the bottom front edge. To avoid this, add ease to the facing by lifting the inner facing ⅛ in. to ¼ in. from the jacket bottom edge before stitching the bottom of the facing to the jacket, as shown in the inset drawing on the facing page.

Add the ½-in.-wide strip of interfacing to "tape" the neck edge and keep it from stretching. Continue stitching the facing to the jacket up to the button location, then center the interfacing strip over the seamline, resin side down. Pull the interfacing to stretch it slightly as you sew to within 1 in. of the shoulder seam. Sew, without pulling, across the back neck, 1 in. past the other shoulder seam. Stretch the remaining interfacing gently as you finish the seam. Fuse the tape to the jacket before you press the seam open. ⇨

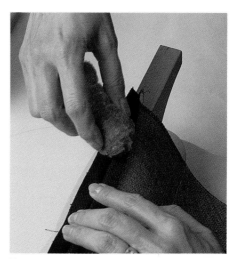

To press open a seam allowance, spread the allowance on a point presser; moisten only the allowance with a dauber (above), and press, lifting the iron rather than sliding it. This is the first step in making a sharp front edge.

Varieties of interfacing (top to bottom): tricot knit, weft insertion, woven cotton, hair canvas, and nonwoven. The top two are most useful in jacket tailoring.

Fusible interfacings

Fusible interfacings have come a long way since their introduction to the home sewer, but interfacing selection can still be confusing. Companies produce similar types, so rather than try to remember brand names, it's easier to learn to identify interfacings by their fabric construction. There are four categories (shown in the photo above): nonwoven, woven, and tricot knit, which may be either fusible or stitch-in; and weft-insertion, which is always fusible. Fusible tricot knit and weft-insertion are the most suitable for today's softly tailored jackets.

Finding the right one

As a general rule, weft-insertion interfacings, which are made from a knitted base with threads added (inserted) across it, will give a firmer hand than the tricot knit. There is also a lightweight version that can be used interchangeably with tricot knit. You aren't limited to only one kind of interfacing in a garment. I often use a lighter weight for facings, hems, and overlay pieces and a firmer weight for the jacket body.

Ideally an interfacing is used to support edges, buttonholes, pockets, collars, and hems without changing the drape of the fashion fabric. Because the resin will add additional body to the fabric after fusing, the only foolproof way to get the right interfacing is to test-fuse it to the fashion fabric.

I keep 3- to 5-yard lengths of each interfacing on hand so I can test each before I begin to cut my garment. It's also more economical than buying small quantities for each project and having unusable scraps left over.

Before cutting, you should preshrink all woven interfacing by soaking it in a basin of hot tap water for about 20 minutes. Blot with a towel and dry the interfacing over the shower rod.

Cut an 8-in. square of fashion fabric and fuse two 3-in.-square interfacing test samples on one half. The unbonded fabric can be folded over the interfacing as a facing, and the two interfacings can be folded together to judge their combined weight. Pink one side of the interfacing squares before fusing to compare with the unpinked side. Pinking will soften the line of the interfacing and help prevent a ridge from forming on the right side of the fashion fabric.

The test sample enables you to compare the drape, surface texture, and color of the interfaced fashion fabric with the original. It also shows you how well the interfacing adheres to the surface. Be careful to check these points on napped or rainwear fabrics and fabrics that waterspot.

Fusing technique

These methods can be used for most interfacings, but check the directions; some manufacturers are now suggesting a dry iron and press cloth rather than steam. The iron must be lifted, moved, and lowered; sliding the iron will distort the interfacing. Place the iron on the interfacing so it overlaps the previously fused area to make sure that the fusing is complete.

To fuse successfully, press the wrong side of the fabric to warm the area that is to be fused. Then place the interfacing on the fashion fabric, wrong sides together. *Be sure the bonding agent is against the fabric.* Use a dampened press cloth, and set the iron to the wool and steam setting. Press for 10 to 12 seconds, lift the iron, and overlap the pressed area liberally with the next press.

Turn the garment section to the right side and repeat the pressing. It's a good idea to use one press cloth when fusing the interfacing to the wrong side and another cloth strictly for the right side. This way, no excess resin will be transferred to the right side of the fashion fabric. – *C.P.*

Pressing and grading seams—To get a sharp front edge on the jacket, you must press the entire front edge seam open before you turn the facing to the inside (shown in the photo at the bottom of p. 31). Press into the hard surface of the point presser and use a clapper to flatten the seam, set the stitches, and crease the seam allowances.

Grade the seam allowances after pressing, trimming the side nearest the body to ¼ in. and the outer allowance to ⅜ in. Remove the excess fabric in the outside curve of the lower edge with pinking shears, and clip the seam allowance in the inside curve of the neckline to make it lie flat.

When you turn the facing to the inside of the jacket, you should find that the garment automatically rolls toward the shorter facing seam allowance. Top-press this seam first from the facing side, using your press cloth, so you can be sure the front edge rolls slightly under to the wrong side of the jacket. Pressing on a cheese block and using a clapper will give you a sharp, professional-looking edge. Finally, top-press the right side of the jacket edges on the cheeseblock. If this pressing flattens the texture of the fabric, dampen a piece of cheesecloth, place it on the right side of the fabric, and off-press (raise the texture) by holding a hot, dry iron just above the cheesecloth; apply no pressure to either fabric. You should hear the water in the cheesecloth sizzle. If you choose to understitch the facing, do it after all underpressing and top-pressing is complete.

Setting the sleeves—I ease the excess fabric in the sleeve cap before setting the sleeve by stitching a bias-cut strip of hair canvas into the sleeve. As the hair canvas relaxes after stitching, it pulls up the sleeve ease evenly. In lightweight wools, the hair canvas will pull too tightly and overease the sleeve, so I use a bias strip of self-fabric or nylon tricot.

Cut a strip of hair canvas on the bias, 1½ in. wide and long enough to reach over the sleeve cap from notch to notch. Beginning at one notch, and using a ½-in. seam allowance, anchor the canvas to the sleeve with a few machine stitches. Stretch the canvas firmly and evenly, as shown in the top photo on the facing page, while you machine baste it to the sleeve, except for ½ in. on each side of the top-of-sleeve notch, where you should not stretch the canvas as you sew.

Once the sleeve has been eased, let it hang freely over the shoulder of your dress form or your curved fingers to check the grain in the cap. Horizontal and vertical yarns should be at right angles to each other, and the sleeve cap should be dimple-free If the horizontal yarns are pulled up toward the top of the sleeve (the usual problem), clip a stitch or two of the easing seam where the yarns are distorted. This should release enough tension to make the yarns straighten. If not, clip more stitches.

Place the cap over a ham and use a dauber to dampen only the seam allowance. With a dry iron at the appropriate temperature for your fabric, shrink out the fullness in the seam allowance by pressing with a lifting and lowering motion. Do not press beyond the stitching line into the crown of the sleeve, and allow the sleeve to dry completely before removing from the ham. Leave the canvas in the sleeve cap to help maintain the sleeve-cap roll and to prevent the seam edge from forming a ridge on the right side of the sleeve.

With the sleeve facing you and the right sides together, pin the sleeve underarm to the jacket from notch to notch, placing the pins parallel to the seamline on the sleeve side. Turn the jacket to the inside, match the center of the sleeve cap to the shoulder seam, and pin the remainder of the sleeve to the armhole. You can now turn the jacket to the right side and check the sleeves for dimples. No hand basting is necessary.

With the wrong side of the jacket against the feed dog and the sleeve on top, machine stitch from one notch, across the underarm to the second notch, and over the sleeve cap. When the entire sleeve has been sewn and you return to your starting point, taper down to a ½-in. seam allowance and restitch the underarm from notch to notch for reinforcement. Trim the underarm seam to ⅜ in. from notch to notch. The hair canvas used for easing often provides enough support, but if the sleeve cap needs more, insert a sleeve head: Cut a strip of needlepunch apparel batting or lamb's wool about 1½ in. wide and 8 in. long (long enough to reach from notch to notch). Centering the strip on top of the sleeve cap, hand baste it to the sleeve seam allowance so it will fold and smooth out the crown when the seam is pressed toward the sleeve.

Top-press the underarm by placing the jacket body over a ham, steaming it, and pressing the seam up (use a press cloth and work from the right side of the jacket). Place the upper part of the sleeve cap over the ham, and finger press the seam allowance toward the sleeve.

Press up the jacket body and sleeve hems and catch-stitch them, using waxed thread for strength.

Insert the lining according to the pattern directions or the method you prefer, then place the front pattern piece on the jacket to mark the buttonhole placement. Push a pin through the pattern tissue at each end of the buttonhole, remove the tissue, and mark the line between the pins.

Most ready-to-wear jackets have a machine-made buttonhole, so don't feel you must have a traditional bound buttonhole. Many new computerized sewing machines make keyhole buttonholes very nicely. If you prefer bound buttonholes, check with tailors and dry cleaners; they will often make them inexpensively. (See *Basics*, No. 37, p. 14, for a hand-worked keyhole buttonhole.)

Open the buttonhole and trim the loose threads. If the interfacing shows in the opening, use a matching felt-tip pen with permanent ink to color the inner edges. For a final touch, use Fray Check to seal the threads.

In making this cardigan jacket, you've mastered a number of contemporary tailoring skills. The next step, the classic jacket with notched collar and welt pockets, is just around the corner. □

Cecelia Podolak is a Clothing Specialist at the University of British Columbia, where she teaches clothing construction and design. She also conducts sewing seminars. Her booklet Pressing Makes a Difference *is available for $6.50 (Can.) from Material Things, 4769 Hoskins Road, North Vancouver, BC V7K 2R3, Canada*

Further reading

Betzina, Sandra. **Power Sewing**. San Francisco: Power Sewing, 1985. *Interfacing, interlining, underlining, lining, and sleeves.*

Betzina, Sandra. **More Power Sewing**. San Francisco: Power Sewing, 1990. *Chest shield.*

Palmer, Pati and Susan Pletsch. **Easy, Easier, Easiest Tailoring**. Portland: Palmer-Pletsch, 1983. *Tailoring fabrics, patch pocket, sleeve setting, lining.*

Sewing for Style. Singer Sewing Reference Library. Minnetonka, MN: Cy DeCosse inc., 1985. *Tailoring with fusible interfacings.*

Tailoring. Singer Sewing Reference Library. Minnetonka, MN: Cy DeCosse inc., 1988. *Explanations and photos of tailoring methods.*

The Perfect Fit. Singer Sewing Reference Library. Minnetonka, MN: Cy DeCosse inc., 1987. *Figure analysis, reference for difficult fitting areas, pin fitting with shoulder pads.*

Easing the sleeve with bias-cut hair canvas *takes two hands, one to guide the fabric layers and one to stretch the canvas. Only ½ in. on either side of the top of the sleeve cap is not stretched.*

Shaping the cap: *With the sleeve cap over a ham, moisten the seam allowance only, then use a dry iron to shrink out the fullness. Be sure not to press beyond the stitching line into the sleeve cap.*

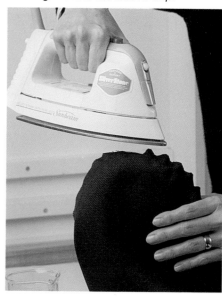

Pressing Matters

A tailor's advice on getting wool into shape

by Katherine Davis

*g*ood pressing and shaping techniques are integral to custom tailoring. Pressing consists of lowering and lifting an iron onto fabric, rather than moving it back and forth as in ironing. In my work as a tailor, I combine pressure, heat, and moisture to shape, shrink, and flatten wool fabric for the carefully sculpted look and thin, flat edges required of a truly well-made woman's garment.

With readily available and relatively inexpensive supplies and equipment and the basic techniques that I'll describe, you will be able to achieve the same results in your own tailoring.

Properties of wool

I'm accustomed to working with wool, which responds beautifully to pressing and is amenable to shaping and shrinking with steam. Wool fabrics are classified as either *woolen* or *worsted*. In woolens, the short fibers in the yarn lie in all directions and produce a fluffy appearance. Worsteds are made with yarns in which the long staple fibers are combed to lie along one direction and short fibers are removed; worsteds are tightly woven cloth commonly found in men's suits.

The amount of heat and moisture required for pressing varies with the type of wool. Softer woolens, such as tweeds, respond well to a combination of a hot *flatiron* and a moistened *presscloth.* (see "Basic pressing equipment" on p. 37 for definitions of italicized terms.) Occasionally they also require the help of a *clapper*. Worsteds, such as tropicals, serges, and gabardines, need a more concentrated effort to flatten edges and always call for the use of a clapper.

Open and flat

Much of the pressing I do is *underpressing,* which is defined as any pressing during coat construction. I use the flatiron with moisture and a presscloth on the inside of the garment or the faced side of edges. If you get into the habit of underpressing each garment section just after you've stitched it, very little *top-pressing,* or final pressing will be needed before the lining is inserted.

Too much pressing is as much a problem as not enough pressing. If you overpress, you might shrink the fabric or change its surface texture.

Good pressing and shaping techiques go hand in hand with sewing in fine tailoring, as shown in this woman's English-cut coat (the tailor's word for a jacket), made by the author from Scottish cheviot wool. Katherine Davis describes her methods in this article.

From *Threads* magazine (April 1991) 34:52-55

Flatiron technique

To show you how to use the flatiron, I'll describe how I press seams (photo sequence at right). Prepare the seam by removing any basting threads that would prevent it from opening completely flat. Always press a seam from the wrong side of the garment so the seam allowances won't show on the right side.

To get the flatiron ready for use, set the heat regulator to high and wait about 10 minutes, then lower it to medium (most woolens require a moderately hot flatiron). Wait yet another 10 minutes before proceeding.

Keep a sponge and a dish of water, or a spray bottle with water handy at the side of the pressboard. Lay the garment on the pressing board, with the lengthwise grainlines running parallel to the board and the seam allowances facing up. Spread the allowances open with your fingers and cover them with a treated *drillcloth* presscloth. Sponge or spray the drillcloth only in the area immediately over the seam allowances.

Lower the hot iron onto the drillcloth, and lift it after waiting just long enough for droplets of water to sizzle and partially evaporate; the drillcloth should still be slightly damp. Lift the drillcloth and pat the garment gently with a *tailor's mitt* to help the seam cool quickly so it won't shrink unnecessarily. Check the right side to be sure that the seam is flat and indiscernible. Continue to press the seam in sections.

For curved garment areas like the hip of a skirt, press the garment over the curves of the *tailor's ham* (see p. 37 for explanation). Never press a curved area on a flat pressboard. Use the same technique I've described, but press in very short sections.

If you're working with a worsted fabric that resists pressing, you might need to *fingerpress* the seam before pressing with the flatiron. To fingerpress, touch moistened fingers to the full length of the opened seam, cover the seam with a moist presscloth, and then press the area.

Working with the clapper

Faced areas, like the collar, bound buttonholes, lapel and front edges, and sometimes stubborn worsted seams, need extra pressure and moisture before they'll lie flat. For this you need a clapper and a wool presscloth.

Prepare the edges for pressing by basting the layers of fabric and interfacing together from the outside into position; I usually use *tailor's basting* or *cross stitching* for basting (see *Basics*, No. 34, p. 20) because they hold the edge more firmly than straight stitches. Baste the faced lapel, for example, along the edge with the ease rolled slightly to the underside. Use silk thread so the basting stitches will not impress the fabric.

Lay the wool presscloth, the garment, and

To press a sleeve seam with a flatiron, Davis lays the sleeve wrong side out on a sleeve board, covers the seam with a drillcloth, and dampens the presscloth over the seam allowances with a sponge that has been dipped into water (top photo). She places the flatiron on the seam allowance (above) and lifts it away when the water beads on the cloth have evaporated, but the presscloth is still damp. To cool the sleeve and prevent shrinking, she lifts the presscloth and pats the sleeve with the tailor's mitt (below).

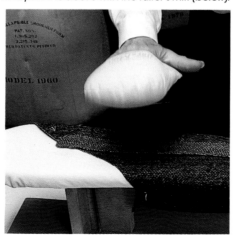

Most edges require the use of a clapper. Davis presses an edge with a clapper immediately after pressing with a flatiron.

the drillcloth, in that order, on the press-board. The wool will preserve the texture of the fabric during firm pressing. Moisten the drillcloth over the edge area. Press with the flatiron, then immediately press hard with the clapper over the same area, as I'm doing in the bottom right photo on p. 35.

Some people feel they need to pound the surface, but it works just as well to press down firmly, putting your weight behind the clapper. (This is why you need a solid, sturdy ironing board!) Hold the clapper down for a second, then release. Pat the area cool with the mitt.

If additional moisture is necessary, you can lightly spray the wool presscloth with water before placing the cloth under the garment. This will further help to prevent flattening of the fabric's surface nap.

Shaping and shrinking

When subjected to moisture and heat, wool felts and shrinks, characteristics the tailor takes advantage of when shaping areas like the collar stand and points, the subtle curve of the lapel into the chest, and the ease in the sleeve cap. When you steam sections, hold the steam iron above the surface of the fabric; never touch the unprotected surface.

Collar—When I build a coat, I prepare the collar separately from the lapel. After the hair canvas interfacing has been pad-stitched to the undercollar, and the under-collar has been stitched to the top collar, I turn the collar with right sides out, and tai-lor baste and press the edges. Then the col-lar is ready for shaping and shrinking along the roll line and at the points.

I pin the completed collar along the largest curve of my custom tailoring ham, which I call a schmoo (see the left photo below), turn-ing the collar down along the roll line. The collar points are pinned down so they will curve inward. I hold the steam iron above the surface and steam along the creased top edge and at both collar points. This process perma-nently sets the shape of the collar roll line. I leave the collar in position until it's thorough-ly dry. Until you're ready to attach the collar to the jacket and to the lapel along the gorge line, never lay it flat; keep it pinned around the ham or a rolled towel.

Lapel—The padstitching that attaches the hair canvas interfacing to the lapel partially shapes it so it will hug the chest of the coat, but I also steam it for a gentle curve that is appropriate for a woman's coat. (A man's tai-lor, in contrast, strives for a very flat look in the lapel and collar sections.) I support the lapel-draped schmoo by the narrow end so the nearly straight edge is up, and carefully steam the lapel (right photo below).

Sleeve cap—After I have carefully pinned the sleeve into the coat, checked the fit on the client, and rotated the sleeve until it's grainline hangs perpendicular to the floor (this is what is meant by balancing a sleeve), I stitch it permanently in place. The sleeve cap is ready to be steamed from the outside. (I never press the armscye seam.) The steaming shrinks the slight amount of extra fullness in the sleeve cap and sets the roundness.

Slip one hand into the pocket of a tailor's mitt and support the coat shoulder with the broad side. Do not extend the mitt into the sleeve cap area. Steam the cap with the iron held in your other hand.

A variation, which I prefer, is to steam the cap while the coat is on a dress form. The garment should be left on a form or hanger while the cap area dries.

Final pressing

After you've finished the coat shell and be-fore you insert the lining, do any top-press-ing that might be necessary, from the right side of the coat. If you're careful to press after each step of construction, and to hang up the parts so they don't wrinkle, your coat will need little or no final pressing.

Place a dry wool presscloth over the gar-ment section, and a dampened drill press-cloth over the wool. Press the coat in small overlapping sections along the directions of the grainlines, in the following order: collar, sleeves, shoulders, facings, jacket front, and jacket back. □

Katherine Davis makes custom suits for women (see Threads, *No. 22), and teaches tai-loring and pattern drafting at 802 Janice Dr., Annapolis, MD 21403; (301) 268-1843. For clapper and sleeve-board construction specifications, send Davis a LSASE.*

Sources

Atlanta Thread & Supply Company
695 Red Oak Rd.
Stockbridge, GA 30281
(800) 847-1001
Rheem flatirons and general equipment. Free catalog; $20 minimum order.

Banasch's
2810 Highland Ave.
Cincinnati, OH 45212
(800) 543-0355
EGT flatirons and general equipment. Free catalog; $25 minimum order.

Cutters Exchange Inc.
4500 Singer Rd.
Murfreesboro, TN 37133
(800) 251-2142;
(800) 342-2500 in TN
Reimers flatirons and general equipment. Call for information. No minimum order but COD only.

Greenberg & Hammer, Inc.
24 West 57th St.
New York, NY 10019
(800) 955-5135
(212)246-2835
General pressing equipment; no flatirons. Catalog upon request; $10 minimum order.

After pinning the collar around the large curve of her custom-made tailor's ham (the schmoo), Davis steams the collar into shape.

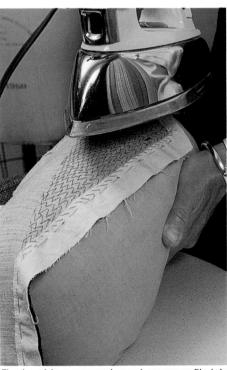

The lapel in a woman's coat curves softly into the coat. To set the curve, drape the interfaced lapel over the schmoo and steam it.

Basic pressing equipment

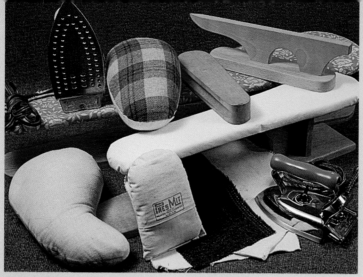

Tools of the trade (clockwise from upper left): a steam iron with plenty of holes in the plate; commercially available tailor's ham; hardwood clapper; point presser with clapper attached; sleeve boards (under steam iron and clapper); American Beauty steamless flatiron; presscloths (wool, twill-woven drillcloth, muslin); tailor's mitt; custom tailor's ham (schmoo).

You may have many of the pressing tools shown at right, but if not, most are easy to obtain from notions and tailoring suppliers (tailoring sources on facing page).

● **Steam iron**—You need a steam iron that provides constant moisture and heat for shaping and/or shrinking. I use an older model Sunbeam that has a "burst of steam" feature. Look for an iron with numerous vent holes.

● **Flatiron**—Also called a *dry iron*, this heavy but versatile iron is steamless, so you must use it with a damp presscloth.

Most tailors choose flatirons that weigh between six and sixteen pounds; I use a six-pound American Beauty that has an oval-shaped pressing area similar to a steam iron. Flatirons also come in a rectangular shape with a blunt, short point. New flatirons cost between $100 and $250, but you can usually pick one up for $10 or less at yard and rummage sales; most people no longer know how to use a flatiron, so they are willing to sell it cheap. Popular professional flatiron brands sold by tailoring suppliers are Reimers, Rheem, or EGT.

Flatirons typically have three temperature settings: low, medium, and high. You'll do most of your pressing with the iron set at low or medium.

● **Presscloth**—Three types of cloth are used for pressing. *Drill*, a dense twill-woven cotton cloth, which often comes chemically treated and packaged ready for pressing, is used with a flatiron. A hot iron pressed down against a dampened drillcloth produces steam. Drillcloth retains moisture and protects the fabric from scorching.

Wool or self-fabric is used for pressing the right side of the fabric. Wool is effective because it protects the surface nap and allows moisture to be driven out of the fabric when beaten by a wooden clapper. I generally use self-fabric if it has a nap.

Muslin is used to press lightweight woolens, but since it is not a good buffer between a hot flatiron and the fabric, you should first test-press a scrap of fabric. Remove all sizing from the muslin by washing it.

● **Pressing boards**—I use two kinds of boards, a large *ironing board* and *sleeve boards*.

The familiar ironing board should be sturdy so it stands up to pressing with a clapper and heavy flatiron. My board is padded with several layers of lambswool and covered with a heavy cotton drillcloth. Good padding prevents seams and edges from imprinting through to the right side of the garment. I don't recommend synthetic ironing board covers because they are impermeable to steam and allow water to condense on the underside of your fabric.

Sleeve boards and pressboards are like small ironing boards and are designed for pressing sleeve and pant seams. They, too, should be well-padded and covered with cotton drillcloth. They can be placed on top of a regular ironing board or on a table during use.

● **Tailor's ham**—The tailor's ham is shaped to approximate body curves. The large arc on the ham is used for setting the collar roll line. The nearly straight edge is used for steaming the lapel area. The small, sharply curved corner is used for pressing the hip area of a skirt, while the darts are pressed on the gently curved ham face.

I prefer my handmade, custom tailor's ham, which I call a schmoo, to the commercially available hams. The store-bought ham, which is often very hard and egg-shaped, lacks the versatility of the softer, multicurved schmoo. My 30-year-old schmoo was made using the pattern shown below as follows: Cut two pairs of the pattern, one of washed muslin, and a second one of washed cotton flannel. Machine stitch the muslin cover around its perimeter except for about three to four inches at the wide end. Fill the ham with kiln-dried sawdust; the drying prevents the sawdust from shrinking after you've sewn it into the ham. Very small, well-dried pieces of cork also work well. Stitch the cover closed by hand. Machine stitch the flannel cover, leaving enough of an opening at the wide end so that you can insert the filled schmoo into it. Finally, stitch the opening closed by hand.

● **Tailor's mitt**—The mitt is used to help cool seams and edges, and to prop up small contoured areas, such as a sleeve cap, for steaming when a dress form is not available. Commercial mitts have wool on one face and a drillcloth pocket on the other. To use, slide your hand into the pocket and wear it like a mitt.

● **Clapper**—Also called a *pounder, block,* or *beater,* the clapper is made of hardwood and is used to force steam out of a just-pressed section and to flatten edges of faced sections of a coat, such as lapels, collars, hems, and front edges.

● **Edge presser or point presser**—The point presser is made of uncovered hardwood and is used to press open the seams of difficult-to-reach areas such as collar points, or the reverse (lapel points) of a jacket. —*K.D.*

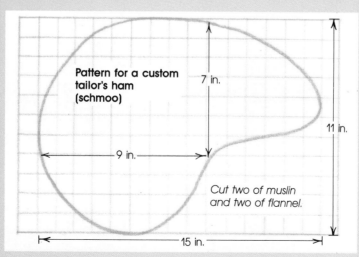

Pattern for a custom tailor's ham (schmoo)

7 in.

11 in.

9 in.

15 in.

Cut two of muslin and two of flannel.

Against the Grain
Exploring the subtleties of couture lapels

by Claire B. Shaeffer

On display in the Costume Court of the Victoria and Albert Museum in London there's an intriguing Ungaro outfit from the mid-'60s. The casual museum visitor might well overlook it, but I took a second look at a clever design feature of that outfit, and it set off a fascination in me that I've been pursuing ever since.

The ensemble, shown in the drawing on the facing page, features a short, double-breasted jacket cut from a horizontally striped fabric. As you can see, the right jacket front folds back to expose the lapel, and the stripes on the lapel facing are parallel to the stripes on the jacket. But if the lapel facings had been cut traditionally, on the lengthwise grain like the garment front, the stripes on the folded lapel would be vertical, interrupting the design. Obviously Ungaro broke with convention for the sake of his design and cut his facing on the crossgrain.

On most ready-made garments and commercial patterns, jacket facings duplicate the grainline of the garment front and are cut so the lengthwise grain is parallel to the center front. Since discovering Ungaro's outfit, I've observed that many tailors and designers manipulate their lapel facings to achieve subtle but wonderful results that home sewers can easily duplicate. The variations usually involve shifting the grain of the facing and/or shaping the straight-cut facing edge to match a curved lapel.

These manipulations are possible regardless of the techniques you're using to construct a jacket front. It doesn't matter whether you're pad-stitching traditional hair canvas by hand, or fusing in the latest weft insertion interfacing (See *Basics*, No. 32, p. 8, for more on fusing to grain-shifted lapels.) As you'll see, these ideas can be applied to any garment that has a fold-over front, not just to traditional tailored jackets based on men's suits. The garments we'll be looking at are all designer garments, ranging from top-of-the-line hand-crafted couture to high quality fused ready-to-wear.

Grain-shifting lapels
By merely rearranging the grain on the facings, striped garments with lapels can be made much more coherent and interesting. The following two designer jackets are not based on men's suits, and the samples were probably made by dressmakers, rather than tailors, in the couturier's workrooms.

Ungaro's solution—In the garment at the V and A, the center front and the garment edge are parallel and they're both on the lengthwise grain. The lower drawing on the facing page shows how Ungaro located the grainline of the facing to be at right angles to the center front. If you're laying out similar pattern pieces, arrange the front first so the color bars are positioned the way you want, then lay out the facing as shown in the drawing, so that the stripes match.

An example from YSL—An Yves Saint Laurent jacket from the Fall/Winter Rive Gauche Collection 1982-83 applies this idea to a slightly more complicated pattern. It's shown in the left-hand group of photos on p. 40, called panel A. This classic Spencer jacket is made from a medium-weight navy wool ottoman. The ottoman fabric has prominent cross ribs, so the crossgrain is easy to identify, and it's easy to see that the edge of the lapel facing is cut on the crossgrain. The garment center is on the lengthwise grain as usual, but the garment edge is not vertical as it was on the Ungaro example.

To duplicate this look on a similar pattern, redraw the lapel grainline so it's perpendicular to the straight edge of the lapel. The left-hand sample in panel A shows a facing cut this way instead of traditionally, with the grain parallel to the center front. The right-hand sample is yet another option; it's cut with the grain parallel to the lapel edge, which positions the crossgrain stripe perpendicular to the stripe on the front when the lapel is folded back.

The ribs on the collar, too, blend beautifully with the ribs on the lapels. Traditionally, jacket collars are cut so that the center back is on the straight grain, parallel to the grain of the jacket's center back. This way, the stripe on a striped jacket can be made to match from collar to back. In the case of the Spencer jacket, the collar has been cut so that its center back is on the *crossgrain*, with the ribs running vertically, instead of horizontally, as on the jacket back. I'd guess that the collar was cut this way so that the ribs didn't cut across the shape of the collar edges, rather than to create the smooth transition at the lapel/collar seam, but both effects are pleasing, and justify the opposing grains at the back of the neck.

Adding shape to shifted lapels
The remaining garments I'll describe are both derived from classic tailored menswear, and both were no doubt made originally by tailors in the designer's workrooms. In each case, the tailor's technique of shaping the lapel facing with an iron to match the curve cut into the garment front has been added to a careful decision about where to place the grain on the lapel.

A couture example from YSL—A daytime ensemble exhibited in the Metropolitan Museum of Art's exhibition of his work (New York City, NY; catalog #203) is a good example of Yves Saint Laurent's consistent attention to detail; it's shown in panel B on p. 40. Designed for the Fall/Winter Couture Collection 1982-83, it features a jacket made from a beige and khaki Prince of Wales plaid with a skirt made from a companion houndstooth check. The jacket is trimmed with houndstooth-check lapels which match the skirt; the check pattern is clearly parallel to the edge of the lapel, but you'll notice that the edge is not parallel to the center front.

I have a duplicate of this garment, so I was able to analyze the garment front and lapel sections and make samples which show the pattern shapes and grainlines quite clearly; they're reproduced in panel B. The grainline on the jacket front is parallel to the center front, not the jacket edge, but the YSL-cut facing on the left is cut with the grainline parallel to the garment edge instead of along the lengthwise grain as usual, like the right-

From *Threads* magazine (December 1990) 32:44-47

hand sample.

The photos in the lower half of panel B show the samples with the lapels folded back. The YSL-cut facing is again on the left. Notice that the garment edge isn't a perfectly straight line, but that the stripe along the edge has been curved to follow the shape. The shaping is subtle, but it keeps the seam from cutting off the stripes.

How it's done—To make a facing pattern for a shaped lapel, use the original pattern as a guide. On pattern paper, or non-woven pattern cloth, draw a straight line near the edge of the pattern material. Lay the facing pattern on the paper so the cutting line touches this line at the widest part of the facing, as shown in the drawing on p. 41, panel C. This is the new cutting line for the facing edge, starting at the curve of the hem. Draw a new grainline parallel to this edge.

Trace the cutting lines at the neckline, shoulder, and lower edge. At the facing edge, transfer the breakpoint (the beginning of the roll line, and usually the beginning of the lapel curve) to the new line and mark it with a notch. If necessary, redraw the inner or unnotched edge so the facing is about 3 in. wide at the shoulder and 6 in. wide at the hem, unless the front edge of the hem is straight; then draw the facing 4½ in. wide at the hem end.

Lay out the new pattern so the vertical bars or stripes will be positioned attractively

Special effect lapels

This mid-60's Ungaro jacket is worth a double take. In order for the lapel stripes to match across the jacket front, the grain of the lapel facing must be arranged to parallel the seam, not the grain, of the front.

Matching stripes on crossgrain facings

Notice where front stripe hits break point and arrange matching facing stripe to hit facing seamline, experimenting to adjust for the turn of the cloth.

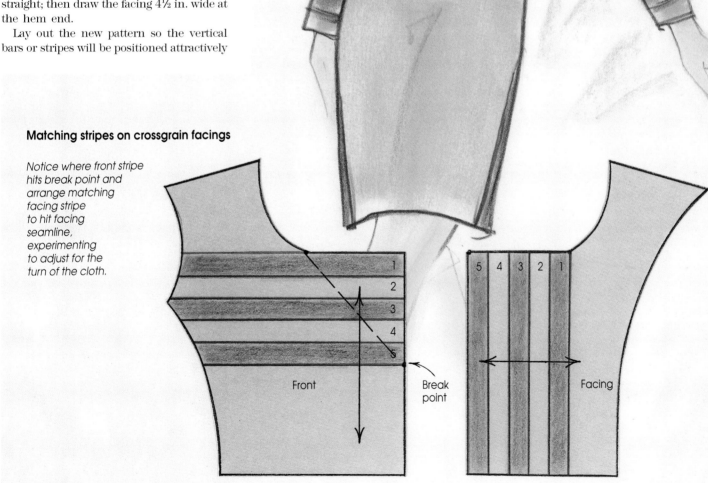

Front

Break point

Facing

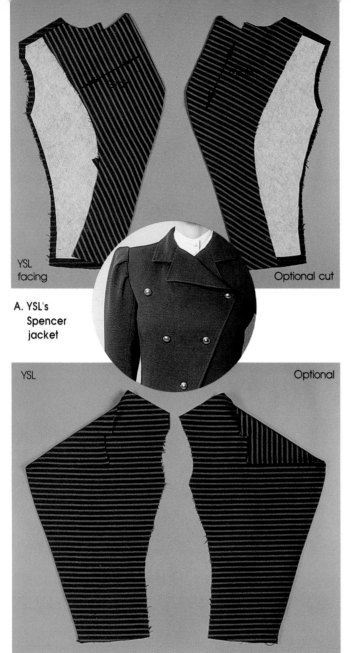

A. YSL's Spencer jacket

YSL facing

Optional cut

YSL

Optional

To continue the horizontal rib across the folded lapel at center, YSL's Spencer jacket has its lapel facings cut like the sample on the left, with grain (this is horizontally-striped fabric) perpendicular to lapel edge; on the right is another option: grain parallel to lapel edge.

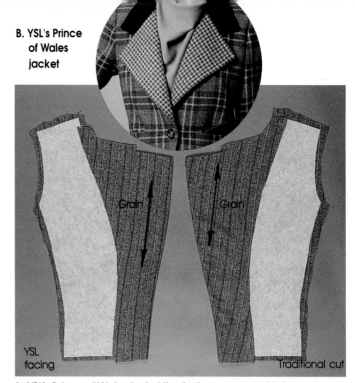

B. YSL's Prince of Wales jacket

Grain   Grain

YSL facing

Traditional cut

In YSL's Prince of Wales jacket the facings are cut with the grain parallel to the lapel edge, instead of parallel to the garment center front. Notice that the YSL lapel has been shaped to follow the curve of the lapel edge, so the stripes don't cut across the lapel seam.

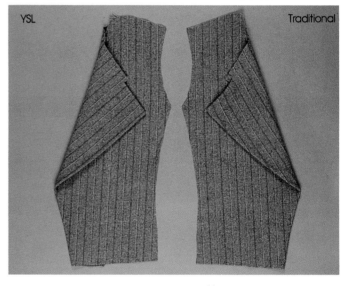

YSL

Traditional

at the lapel edge. I like a dominant bar at the edge; but I've learned that if I lay out the pattern so the seamline is exactly on the edge of the color bar, I will lose some of the bar in the turn of the cloth. I've also found that, when cutting, it is safer to wait until after I've shaped the front edge to cut the neckline. At this stage I cut the facing straight across from the edge to the cutting line of the shoulder seam.

Once you've cut out the two facings, you'll need a guide to help you shape the facings accurately to the garment front. In *Classic Tailoring Techniques: A Construction Guide for Women's Wear* (by Cabrera and Meyers, Fairchild Publications, NY; 1984) the authors recommend that

you draw the curve from the front pattern on paper, pin the paper to your pressing board, and use it as a guide until you can trust your eye to duplicate the jacket curve.

Lay the facings on the pressboard so the neckline is toward your right and the unnotched inner edge is toward you. With your left hand, hold the edge of the facing at the breakpoint. Then, beginning at the neckline, move the iron in an arc counterclockwise with your right hand while your left hand gently pulls the facing toward you to form a convex curve at the edge, as in the top photo on the facing page. Start with large arcs at the outer edge, and as you work toward the inner edge use smaller arcs to shrink away the excess and avoid unwanted creases.

As you shape the lapel into a convex curve, ripples will form along the unnotched inner edge of the facing. Shrink them away so the lapel will maintain its new shape. This sounds much more difficult than it is. Wool is the easiest fabric to shape; and woolens and/or loosely woven fabrics are easier to shape than worsteds and hard-finished materials, like the wool ottoman used in the Spencer jacket shown above. Perhaps this is why the facing on the Spencer jacket wasn't shaped.

When I'm sewing the front to the facing of a man-tailored garment such as this, I hand-baste both facings and edges together, steam press just the basted seamlines, then turn the seams right side out to be sure they are perfect and identical. Finally, with the right sides together, I machine-stitch the seamlines.

Yet more subtleties—The Rive Gauche plaid jacket from Fall/Winter 1984-85 in the photo at bottom right may be the most exciting garment in my collection; and I am even more impressed because it is from the ready-to-wear, not the couture, collection. The facings on this jacket are not only shaped, like the lapels described above, as you can see in the center left photo, but the plaid on the facing is moved up so it meets the corresponding color bar on the front when it is folded open, as you can see in the photo at center right. When most tailored garments are made from a plaid or horizontal stripe, the facing is applied to the front so the patterns are matched at the front/facing seamline which joins them. When this is done, the bars on the lapel always fall below the same bars, on the front. For this design, Saint Laurent has moved the facing up so the bars are positioned more attractively when the lapel is rolled into place. In this case, the facing was moved up 1¼ in., but the exact amount will of course vary with the fabric, the garment design, and the lapel roll.

To duplicate this effect, don't cut out the facings until you've first established the position of the plaid on the facing by pinning the paper pattern to a finished front. Prepare at least one garment front, either by hand-padding the lapel, and taping the roll line and front edge; or with speed-tailoring methods, if that's the way you're constructing your garment. If you haven't already, make a new facing pattern, as shown in the drawing at right. Then, on both the facing pattern and garment front, baste the seam allowances at the lapel edge under. Match the folded edges and pin them together. Fold the lapel to its finished position, and carefully mark where the horizontal bars on the front meet the facing edge.

I pin a small scrap of plaid (approximately 1 in. wide X 4 in. long) in place on the facing pattern so I won't get confused when I remove the pattern from the garment; I lay it out for cutting, right side up, on a single layer of fabric. To make sure the plaids are just right and positioned identically, I cut out just one facing, and pin it to the front to check that it falls the way I want. If everything looks good, I turn the first facing face down on my fabric and chalk around it to cut its mate, shape them both to match the front curve, and permanently join them to the garment. □

Claire B. Shaeffer teaches couture techniques at Eastern Michigan University every summer. For more information, contact E. Rhodes, E. M. U., Ypsilanti, MI 48197.

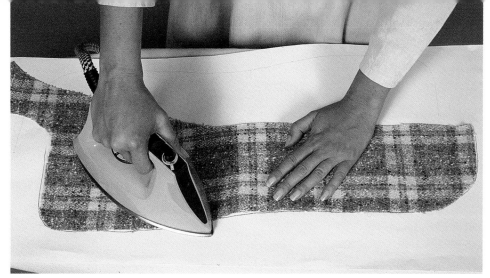

To shape the lapel facing, work towards the inside edge, and iron in decreasing arcs to curve the far edge outward. As you move the iron with one hand, pull the facing into shape with the other.

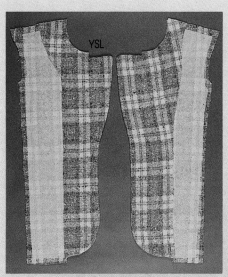

In YSL's 1985 gray plaid jacket, the facings are again shaped to follow the curve, but the plaid has also been arranged so that it matches the position of the plaid on the jacket front when the lapel folds open, instead of matching along the seam line as usual.

Redrawing a facing pattern for a shaped lapel

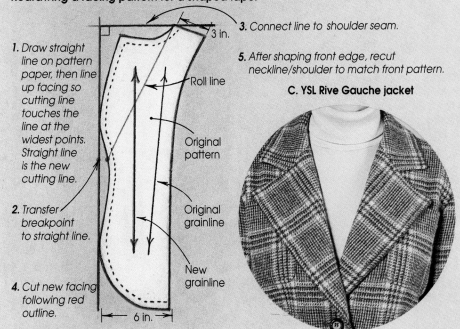

1. Draw straight line on pattern paper, then line up facing so cutting line touches the line at the widest points. Straight line is the new cutting line.

2. Transfer breakpoint to straight line.

4. Cut new facing following red outline.

3 in.

3. Connect line to shoulder seam.

5. After shaping front edge, recut neckline/shoulder to match front pattern.

Roll line

Original pattern

Original grainline

New grainline

C. YSL Rive Gauche jacket

6 in.

Facing Finesse

A couture waistband thins even the thickest fabrics

by Claire B. Shaeffer

according to the Duchess of Windsor, you can never be too rich or too thin. Unlike the Duchess, most of us have added a few inches here and there. My extra inches tend to accumulate around my waist, so I'm always looking for designs that make it look smaller. A couture waistband appears to shave a couple of those unattractive inches because it reduces fabric bulk; it's also comfortable to wear even when the skirt or trouser is made of scratchy or bulky fabric.

Technically, the couture band is just a faced waistband, as shown in the photo at right. The outside of the band is made of self-fabric while the layer next to your body is a slipstitched lining-fabric facing. Only two layers of fashion fabric—one from the skirt and one from the band—are stitched into the waist seam; the interfacing is not stitched into any seam.

The faced band can be used for almost any design—straight or shaped, narrow or wide. It is great for wide bands because its top edge can be stretched and steamed into shape to fit a larger-than-average rib cage smoothly. Generally, this band isn't appropriate for washable garments.

The couture waistband, thinner and smoother than any you'll find on a ready-made garment, is cut and sewn for a custom fit. Because it is assembled and stitched mainly by hand and applied temporarily for fitting, the couture band can be adjusted for individual figure irregularities without difficulty.

It's not my intention in this article to tell you how to fit the skirt or trousers, but they need to be at least basted together so you can check the waistband's fit. (The garment will hang better if you fold the basted seams and darts to one side and baste them flat.) Baste the hem up, and baste the seam allowances under at the zipper placket.

The zipper won't be inserted until the band is stitched permanently in place. Mark the garment centers, side seams, and waistline with chalk or thread tracing (hand-sewn running stitches). You'll use these marks to accurately place the band.

Just the right support

Hair canvas and petersham, a very crisp grosgrain ribbon with distinct scalloped edges, work well as interfacings because they can be shaped easily with heat and moisture. You can also use any crisp, lightweight sew-in or fusible interfacing that will maintain its shape when the garment is worn. Some of the interfacings I like are Armo Press Firm, Formite II, Sew-In Durapress, Bridal Shape, and regular grosgrain ribbon. Nonwoven interfacings and many of the popular woven waistband stiffenings aren't flexible enough to use for this technique.

To select just the right interfacing, I first analyze the design and experiment with interfacing scraps I have on hand. Wide or shaped bands need a crisper interfacing than straight, narrow bands; petersham, because of it's ribbed, grosgrain texture, can only be used for straight or nearly straight bands. A crisp, firm waistband usually requires at least two layers of interfacing; when two fabric layers aren't crisp enough, I add another. When three layers of the same interfacing are too bulky, I might try layers of two different interfacings, such as a layer of sew-in with a layer of fusible or two layers of fusible.

Preshrink the interfacing before it is applied. I usually preshrink mine immediately after it's purchased so that when I experiment, I know exactly how stiff it will be in the finished garment. You may prefer to sew or fuse the interfacing layers together, then shrink them.

To preshrink sew-in interfacings, press

The couture waistband of this Chanel fabric skirt is faced with soft silk charmeuse. The silk is more comfortable next to the skin than scratchy wool fabric. The waistband technique the author describes is superb for bulky fabrics.

them with lots of steam; to preshrink fusibles, soak them in hot water for ten minutes, press out the excess water, and hang them to drip dry. If you'd rather fuse the layers first, cover the fused layers with a damp cloth and press.

The same technique that I use to prepare hair canvas interfacing can be applied to any of the interfacings I've mentioned. Cut a strip of interfacing at least 3 in. wide and about 5 in. longer than your waist measurement. Fold the strip in half lengthwise and zigzag about ¼ in. from the folded edge (stitch width 4 mm, stitch length 2 mm). Continue quilting the layers together with zigzagged rows spaced about ¼ in. apart, always beginning at the same end. This quilting makes the interfacing crisper without adding bulk. It's faster to straight stitch; however, the band will be slightly more difficult to shape and it won't be as crisp.

Since I often need hair canvas interfacing, I cut a length of canvas at full width and quilt the entire piece. Whether you prepare one band interfacing or many, cut off the fold and the selvages after quilting.

I don't leave folds in because they create an inflexible area of fabric, which defeats any shaping I might need to do. I remove selvages for the same reason.

Fabric for the outside

To determine the waistband length to cut from the fashion fabric, start with your waist measurement and add 5 in. This length allows for two ½ in. seam allowances and 3 in. for an overlap/underlap. It also includes ½ in. to 1 in. of ease for a more comfortable fit; some of this ease will be lost because of the

From *Threads* magazine (August 1990) 30:64-67

Preparing the band for fitting

1. Cut waistband fabric and thread trace seamlines at center front, back, and at the sides.

2. Baste trimmed and quilted interfacing to band.

	Thread tracing
	Machine zigzagging
	Basting

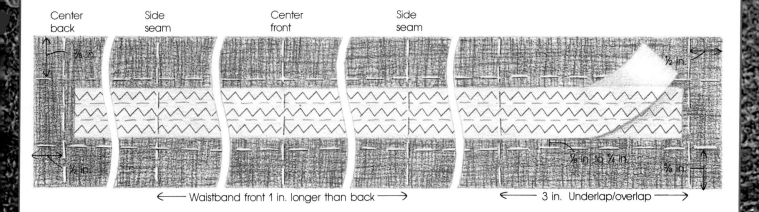

Center back   Side seam   Center front   Side seam

⅜ in.

½ in.

½ in.

⅛ in. to ¼ in.

⅝ in.

← Waistband front 1 in. longer than back →

← 3 in. Underlap/overlap →

3. Wrap band seam allowances around interfacing and baste in place.

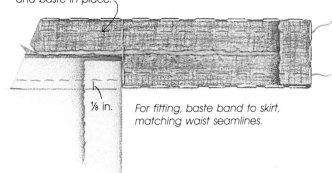

⅛ in.

For fitting, baste band to skirt, matching waist seamlines.

Interfacing trimmed too much

Thread tracing shows on reverse side.

Interfacing not trimmed enough

Thread tracing shows on outside.

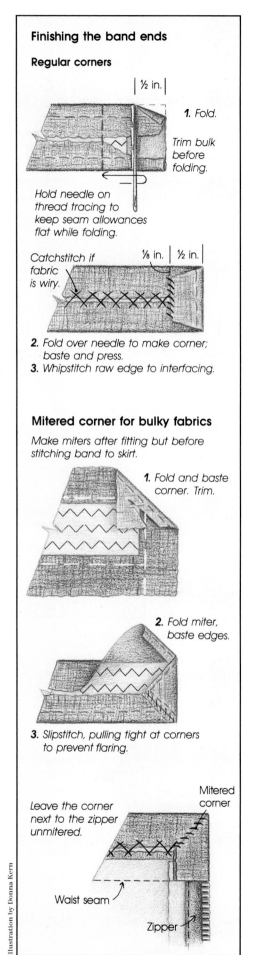

Finishing the band ends

Regular corners

1. Fold.

| ½ in. |

Trim bulk before folding.

Hold needle on thread tracing to keep seam allowances flat while folding.

Catchstitch if fabric is wiry.

| ⅛ in. | ½ in. |

2. Fold over needle to make corner; baste and press.

3. Whipstitch raw edge to interfacing.

Mitered corner for bulky fabrics

Make miters after fitting but before stitching band to skirt.

1. Fold and baste corner. Trim.

2. Fold miter, baste edges.

3. Slipstitch, pulling tight at corners to prevent flaring.

Leave the corner next to the zipper unmitered.

Mitered corner

Waist seam

Zipper

Illustration by Donna Kern

---

turn of the fabric at the seams.

For the band width, add two ⅝ in. seam allowances to the desired finished width. Bands generally are finished 1 in. to 1¼ in. wide, although a band that is used as a design element can be any size or shape. I prefer the 1-in. width for comfort because my rib cage extends to my waist, and I add only ½ in. for seam allowances.

The interfaced waistband won't stretch out of shape, so you can cut it on the cross grain or lengthwise grain. I've rarely seen a couture bias waistband.

The band needs to be marked as accurately as possible to make it easier to fit and stitch. Using chalk or pastel thread tracing, mark the seamlines at the top, bottom, and ends of the waistband, as shown in the top drawing on p. 43. I like thread tracing because it's easy to see on both sides of the fabric and won't rub off like chalk when handled. Avoid bright, intense, or dark thread colors—the color may rub off the thread and leave a permanent stain on the fabric. Before you mark the band's centers and side seams, decide whether you prefer an overlap, an underlap, or both. For an underlap, for example, the marked seamline on one end of the band will be aligned with the folded edge of the zipper placket; the other end of the band will be marked 3 in. from the edge of the placket. If you're not sure where to mark the side seams, a good rule of thumb is that the front waist measurement is 1 in. longer than the back waist.

Cut a strip of quilted interfacing ⅛ in. to ¼ in. smaller on all sides than the finished dimensions of the band. For most fabrics, ⅛ in. allows for the turn of the cloth, but heavier fabrics may require a ¼ in. trim.

Place the interfacing on the wrong side of the waistband. Pin and hand baste it to the band. If the interfacing is the correct width, each seam allowance will wrap around the interfacing so that the chalked line or thread tracing is right on the edge, (lower left drawing, p. 43). If it's too wide, the marked line will show on the right side of the band (lower right drawing, p. 43); if it's too narrow, the line will show on the underside. Wrap all seam allowances around the interfacing and baste them in place.

If the band is shaped, you'll need to cut the interfacing using the waistband pattern and trim ⅛ in. from each edge. Before basting it to the waistband, pin it in place and check to see if you need to trim more.

To set the fibers of the interfacing and fabric so that they grab together, press the band flat with the interfacing up, using lots of steam. If the band is narrow, use the iron to stretch the upper edge about ½ in. so that it will fit the rib cage smoothly. For a band wider than 1½ in., stretch it more.

If the top of the band falls at the waistline, stretch the lower edge of the band.

Fitting exactly

Now you're ready to check the fit of the band. With the skirt and band right sides up, match the lower edge of the band to the seamline at the skirt waist; align and pin the match points at the garment centers and side seams. Pin the band in place so that the skirt is eased smoothly. Baste the band in place using short, even basting stitches about ⅛ in. from the lower edge.

Try on the skirt, lapping and pinning the band ends so that the match points are aligned; the opening will have to be pinned closed because the skirt zipper is not yet in place. The band should fit smoothly. If it rolls, the interfacing isn't crisp enough; if it has wrinkles at the sides, the top of the band may be too tight for the rib cage.

Occasionally the band will roll because it is too tight or the fabric is unusually bulky. Repin the band so it is comfortable, using some of the 3 in. overlap/underlap. Remove the band and re-mark the centers and side seams before basting it back on the skirt.

If you need to make any corrections, use a different pastel color for the new thread tracing than the one used originally so that it's easy to tell which thread tracings are the final markings. For example, I use light yellow instead of white for the first set of corrections and pink thread for any second corrections.

When the fitting is finished, you're ready to stitch the band permanently in place. (If the fabric is bulky and requires mitered corners, make the miters as described in the drawing at left before stitching the band in place.) Remove the band from the skirt and the basting that holds the seam allowances in place from the band's lower edge and ends. Remove only enough basting from the top edge of the band to release the ends. If you want to reduce the bulk in the overlap/underlap, trim the interfacing so it extends only 2 in. beyond the zipper placket. With right sides together, baste the band on the skirt, matching the seamlines and match points, and stitch it by machine permanently; this is the only machine stitching in the band. Fasten the threads at each end with a tailor's knot and remove the basting from the waist seam. Press the seam flat (unopened) to set the stitches but don't press the ends; then press both seam allowances toward the band as shown in the left photo above. Trim the skirt seam allowance to ⅜ in. so that its edge doesn't coincide with the edge of the ⅝-in. seam allowance of the band. When the fabric is very bulky, press the seam open except for a 2-in. portion on the unlapped end of the band which is still pressed toward the

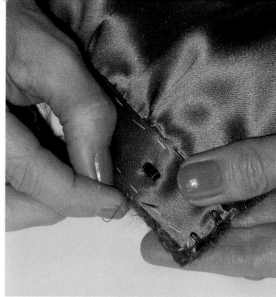

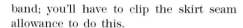

Shaeffer irons the machine-stitched waist seam in the band, carefully avoiding the ends (left). She carefully stitches the silk facing in place with fell stitches (above). The folded edge on the end is tucked under the anchoring loops of the hooks. The third hook was slipped through a hole in the lining she made with an awl without breaking any threads.

band; you'll have to clip the skirt seam allowance to do this.

Nice, neat corners

On lightweight and medium weight fabrics, the band corners can be finished without miters. Baste the seam allowances on the band's lower edge to the wrong side. Press the bottom and the top folds of the band (the top seam allowance is still basted), but don't press the ends. If the seam allowances lap at the center of the band, trim them.

You can trim away some of the bulk before folding, and since you haven't ironed the ends yet, you can taper them slightly to make a neater corner. Fold the ends over a needle to the wrong side (as shown in the top drawing on the facing page) along the thread tracing, and baste them in place with a soft cotton thread or size A silk thread; either thread will not leave an impression when ironed. Press the folded ends, using a damp press cloth, and spank them briskly with a clapper to flatten them.

At the raw ends, trim away any stray threads. Tack the ends lightly through the fashion fabric to the interfacing with small whipstitches. If the fabric is wiry, catch-stitch the long seam allowance edges flat.

When the fabric is just too bulky to fold neatly at the corners, you'll have to miter three of the corners; the lower corner on the overlap/underlap can usually be finished flush with the zipper placket without a miter, as shown in the bottom drawing on the facing page.

Before stitching the band to the skirt, but after fitting, remove all band bastings

except those holding the interfacing in place, open the seam allowances, and press the band ends flat. At the three corners, fold the corner seam allowance to the wrong side, as shown in the center drawing on the facing page; baste close to the fold-line, press, and trim away the corner. Fold and baste the seam allowances so that the folded edges meet to form a miter at each corner (second drawing from the bottom, facing page). Slipstitch the folded edges together. To avoid "rabbit ears" right at the corner, be sure your thread is anchored well and pulled taut.

Finishing up

The band is almost ready for the facing. Set the skirt zipper by hand and sew the skirt lining, if any, to the band with short running stitches in the seam allowance only, placed about ⅛ in. above the waist seam.

For security, I like to use three or four sets of the large fur or coat hooks and eyes, instead of heavy skirt hooks. At this point, you can add eyes to the outside of the underlap and two hooks to the edge of the overlap. The innermost hooks can be stitched to the band through all layers after the facing is in place. I prefer to sew all hooks on, and then make holes in the facing with an awl to slip the hooks through, as I did for the skirt in the photo on p. 43. The awl pushes threads aside, rather than cutting them.

On the right side of the underlap, sew two eyes about 1 in. from the end of the band and two more about ⅛ in. from the opening. On the wrong side of the overlap, sew two

hooks about ⅛ in. from the end and one or two more 1 in. from the end and anchor them securely so that the hooks won't show when the band is stressed.

To face the waistband, first cut a strip of lining ¾ in. longer and wider than the finished waistband. If the lining is a satin-weave fabric, cut the strip on the length-wise grain for stability; otherwise, it doesn't matter whether it's cut lengthwise or crosswise.

With wrong sides together, center the facing strip over the waistband; pin them and baste at the center. Turn under the raw edges of the facing at the top and ends so that the edges are ⅛ in. from the edges of the band. At the end of the overlap, tuck the folded edge under the hooks (as in the right photo above). Pin and baste the facing in place. To avoid catching my thread on the pins, I only pin a few inches at a time in front of my basting. Also, I set the pins at an angle so that I can pull them out easily.

Turn under the raw edge at the waistline so that the facing barely covers the stitched line that anchors the skirt lining; pin and baste. Press the facing lightly. Use small fell stitches to secure the lining. Remove all bastings, and sew the remaining two hooks onto the overlap if you didn't add them earlier. □

Claire B. Shaeffer, who described the beautiful work of Zandra Rhodes in Threads, *No. 29, teaches couture techniques at the College of the Desert in Palm Desert, CA and at Eastern Michigan University in Ypsilanti, MI.*

Issey Miyake: Designer for the Millennium

Fold and finish your own versions from commercial patterns

by Marcy Tilton

i f I could wear the clothes of only one designer, the decision would be easy: Issey Miyake. His clothes are classics in the true sense of the word. They belong to a time all their own and can be worn by anyone, regardless of age, figure type, or gender. Miyake's fans are legion and diverse, ranging from jazz trumpeter Miles Davis to designer Giorgio Armani.

Miyake is one of a handful of designers who contracts with Vogue Patterns to provide patterns of selected items from his ready-to-wear line. I am a passionate and prolific sewer. To me, the acid test for a successful garment is its longevity in my active wardrobe. The only garments that have made it beyond two years are Miyake's. I'm still wearing clothes I made from the very first Vogue Issey Miyake pattern.

I always make it a point to look at Miyake's ready-to-wear collection for ideas and inspiration, and to get a feeling for his themes and motivations, but I never "copy" or even attempt to re-create them exactly. One of the reasons I enjoy working with his shapes and designs is that I become stimulated and excited about making them work for me—my life, my figure, and the fabrics that I find. I wear his clothes almost every day; some are very knock-around casual, some are perfect for business, others make just the right statement for lectures and presentations, and some I save for evening and dressy occasions.

Issey Miyake clothing is fun to make and wear. Each garment can function as a building block in any wardrobe. I buy all the patterns because the designs have a longevity and style that no other designer's clothes have, and the pieces from different patterns often work with one another. Like old friends, the patterns become better and better and more fun with use and experience. I've shortened a dress pattern to make a spectacular top, lengthened a jacket pattern to make a raincoat, modified the long sleeves of a blouse to make a camp shirt, and added a belt and buttons to pleats. Miyake's clothes give your taste and personal style room to grow and change, for he is usually ahead of and beyond the fashion game.

I'd like to share what I've learned about appropriate fabrics to use, characteristics you're likely to see in Miyake's designs, and the sewing challenges the designs create so that you can make some really wonderful versions of your own.

Yours for the sewing: Miyake Vogue patterns encompass the unusual details and cuts of his ready-to-wear. The author created the suit at far left from a 1990 pattern but took cues for fabrics and textures from Miyake's retail garments, like the pleated jacket from the 1991 Plantation line. (Photo by Yvonne Taylor)

Designs that stand alone

Miyake produces a high-priced, ready-to-wear collection for women, Issey Miyake Boutique; a less expensive collection called Plantation; collections for men; and a coat collection labeled Windcoat. He recently created the Permanente collection, a concept that has no precedent in the fashion business, which showcases his best vintage designs and favorites from previous collections.

The quality of Issey Miyake ready-to-wear is that of fine handsewn clothing without the pretense of couture. Everything is finished beautifully inside and out, but has an easy feel. In Miyake's ready-to-wear, seams and edges are always finished. French seams, flat-fell seams, turned-and-stitched seams, bound seams, and topstitching are all used to maximum effect. Serging is discreet, subtle, and usually narrow.

There are several themes that recur in Miyake's ready-to-wear lines as well as in his Vogue patterns. Many of the designs start as rectilinear shapes that Miyake drapes on the body, and although the garments are often oversized, they reveal the human form. These designs magically adjust to fat or skinny bodies.

Miyake is fond of pleats and folds as design elements in their own right, but he also uses them unpredictably to mold and shape rectangular shapes. Asymmetrical design elements abound, which means sewers must lay out pattern pieces carefully and cut them singly. Overlaid pieces and *origami* (the art of Japanese paper folding) influences are other trademarks.

Similar neckline and cowl variations occur again and again. Miyake likes to cut the collars and lapels of shirts, jackets, and coats as part of the garment's front, as he did for the jackets at left. This cut often requires skill at insetting square pieces of fabric, which I'll discuss in a bit.

Pockets and their placement are always considered carefully and are integrated with the overall design. Mitered corners are frequently used both as a design element and to reduce bulk. Closures may be unconventional and are sometimes reminiscent of kimono ties. Miyake's patterns have called for closures such as drawstrings threaded through buttonholes, hand lacing, and braided ties.

Fabric first

Miyake firmly believes that design begins with fabric. He works with cloth the way a sculptor works with clay: He smells it, squeezes it, carefully examines both sides, and creates his designs by wrapping and draping, referring to this process as "manual labor." He has used quilted cottons; basket-woven straw; ikats; and Japanese tie-dyed, puckered, and paper cloth. He has

used fabric he describes as "whisker" linen, "downy hair," and "dobby" doubleweave linen. Like Chanel, early in his career he took a wool jersey and turned it into outerwear. Miyake has even made garments with rubber, plastic, metal, bamboo, and stones.

Miyake loves stripes and has spent years researching and designing striped fabrics. A favorite fabric of his has textured stripes on one side and a solid color on the other. Any fabric that is double-faced seems to intrigue Miyake, and it turns up again and again in his ready-to-wear.

Miyake works with some of the world's finest textile designers, weavers, and craftspeople, and together they develop new textile designs from images of daily life and from the surrounding environment. He has been said to be just as interested in a weaver's "mistakes" because he finds them inspiring.

If Issey Miyake has some of the finest textiles in the world at his disposal, what are the options for home sewers? Bear in mind that Miyake usually selects natural colors. Also note that although textured and handwoven fabrics are associated with his designs, they are usually limited to simple shapes and serve as focal points within an ensemble: scarves, coats, vests, jackets. Basic garments such as skirts, tops, and pants are often constructed of simple wool jersey, wool and rayon crepe, cotton, or linen. So combine textured pieces with plain weaves.

Handwoven and unusual fabrics (see *Supplies*, No. 35, p. 28) are perfect for many Miyake designs. You can also try creating your own puckered fabric by spinning and weaving (see "Make Your Own High-Fashion Fabric," No. 35, pp. 38-39) or by experimenting with commercially available wools, wool blends, and natural/synthetic blends. Try this technique, which artists call "stressing" the fabric. Test an eighth-yard of fabric first. Put the fabric in hot water—this can felt it—then immerse it in cold water, which might alter it again. You might try throwing the sample into the washing machine and agitating it, then see what effect machine drying gives. Blends of natural and synthetic fibers may react differently—one may shrink and the other may not.

Every season Miyake comes out with a line of white shirts in fine cotton, linen, or silk. Make any Miyake blouse pattern in your best white fabric, and you'll have the garment for the rest of your life.

Fitting: start of the puzzle

Even though Miyake's designs are proportioned to look good on all types of figures, I strongly suggest that you fit and pretest the pattern and sewing techniques. The more loosely fitted the garment, the easier it will be to fit. As fashion and styles have moved closer to the body, so have some of Miyake's patterns, and these fitted or semi-fitted garments require some preliminary fitting work.

Miyake's pattern pieces often look like no others and may be confusing at first. (Look at the blouse cut in the sketch below to see what I mean). Even if you are accomplished at sewing and fitting, start by examining the pattern pieces and reading the directions *completely* before you begin the fitting process.

Pin fitting is a must—it shows what the garment looks like and will give you an idea of how it is assembled, as well as how it will fit and which alterations are necessary. Pin fitting is the next best thing to trying on the actual garment, and while it takes a bit of practice to go at it with confidence, it is a practical and painless fitting tool. It works best on tops, blouses, jackets, and coats; it is difficult (but not impossible) for pants and some skirts.

It may take you some time to get accustomed to "seeing" the garment during pin fitting. You must be careful when trying a pin-fit garment on so it hangs properly.

To pin fit, pull out the main pattern pieces—front, back, sleeve. Pin the body pieces together with pins parallel to and right on the seamlines and with the seam allowances on the outside. Try the sleeve on separately. Look at the overall proportions, length, pocket placement, seam, and detail placement. The fact that these patterns seem to be oversized may be misleading; often the "extra" fabric is taken up in a design detail, like a pleat, or is simply necessary for the right effect, so be careful not to confuse fitting ease with design ease.

Alterations

If you are accustomed to making particular alterations to all Vogue patterns, do them before pin fitting if possible. Do any length alterations first, then the width alterations. *Always make your changes following the grainlines.* Since many of Miyake's designs

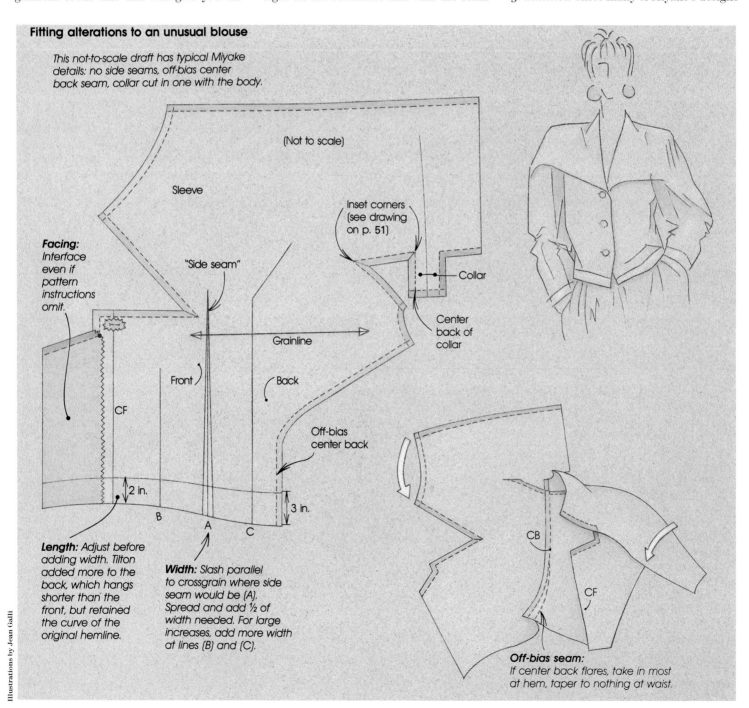

Fitting alterations to an unusual blouse

This not-to-scale draft has typical Miyake details: no side seams, off-bias center back seam, collar cut in one with the body.

(Not to scale)

Sleeve

Inset corners (see drawing on p. 51)

Collar

Center back of collar

Facing: Interface even if pattern instructions omit.

"Side seam"

Grainline

Front

Back

CF

Off-bias center back

2 in.

B   A   C

3 in.

Length: Adjust before adding width. Tilton added more to the back, which hangs shorter than the front, but retained the curve of the original hemline.

Width: Slash parallel to crossgrain where side seam would be (A). Spread and add ½ of width needed. For large increases, add more width at lines (B) and (C).

CB

CF

Off-bias seam: If center back flares, take in most at hem, taper to nothing at waist.

Illustrations by Jean Galli

are based on rectangles, you can often easily add or subtract length or width parallel to the sides.

No side seams—Some Miyake patterns have no side seams. So if you need to widen or narrow the garment, you have to draw in a side seam, slash along the seam, and spread the pattern, using the grainline as a guide. I've shown how I modified a blouse pattern in the left drawing on the facing page.

Bias seams—Miyake sometimes designs garments that place the center back seam on an odd off-bias. I've seen this characteristic in dresses, jackets, and shirts. Miyake and his staff usually work by draping fabric on a mannequin, and they work out the stretch and slight distortion that occurs along a bias seam in that sample fabric; you may have to adjust the bias seam as you work in your fabric. I have found that garments with such a seam tend to become too wide, and that the center back seam sometimes requires taking in, starting with the greatest amount at the hem and tapering to nothing just above the waist (see the lower right drawing opposite). The amount of extra is determined by your fabric; it is not a pattern "problem," but a matter of fine-tuning the fit. It is helpful to be aware of this before finishing the hem.

Circular skirts—Circle skirts are another favorite Miyake theme, but his versions at first glance may not even resemble a "normal" version of a circle skirt (see the center drawings on p. 50). Altering these styles should be done at the waist, rather than by splitting the pattern, so you retain the skirt's design proportions.

Fold and pin the skirt pieces together so the pattern resembles the final skirt, and compare the measurement of your waist with that of the pattern. Lay the measuring tape on its side, and measure directly on the seamline, omitting darts, tucks, and pleats. The skirt waist should measure 1½ in. to 2½ in. larger than your waist, less for slim figures, more for full figures. If you deepen the seamline 1 in. or more, you also may want to add to the skirt length and reposition markings.

It takes surprisingly little widening to increase the waist a lot. Begin by redrawing the waistline diameter ¼ in. larger into the skirt body and remeasure the seamline. If

Miyake's clever use of folds is apparent in two eye-catching suits. At near right is a wool crepe version of Vogue pattern 2428, made by author Marcy Tilton. The jacket of double-faced linen at far right, from the Spring/Summer '91 Plantation line, has carefully mitered edges and flat-fell seams. (Photo by Yvonne Taylor)

Altering the waist of a circular skirt

Standard skirt:
Increase waist by increasing the waist circle diameter.

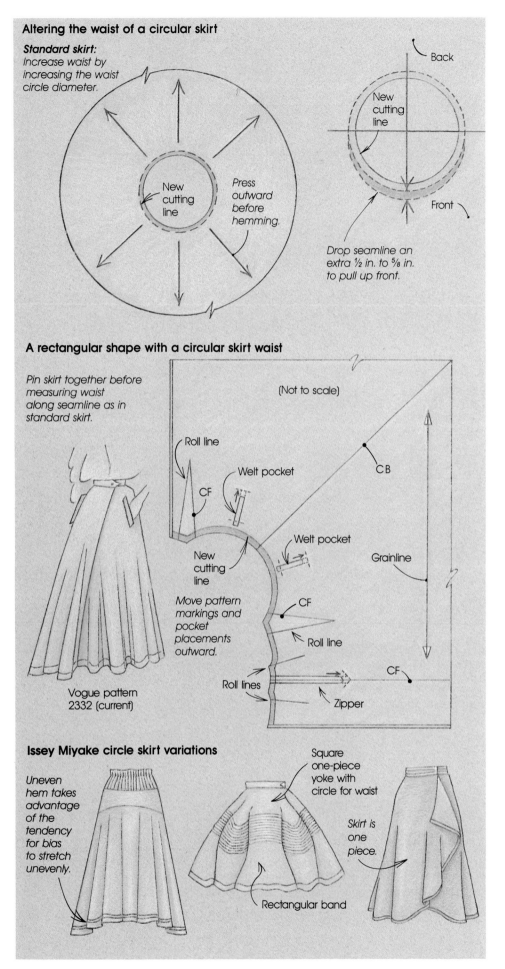

New cutting line

Press outward before hemming.

Back

New cutting line

Front

Drop seamline an extra ½ in. to ⅝ in. to pull up front.

A rectangular shape with a circular skirt waist

Pin skirt together before measuring waist along seamline as in standard skirt.

(Not to scale)

Roll line

Welt pocket

CF

CB

Welt pocket

New cutting line

Grainline

Move pattern markings and pocket placements outward.

CF

Roll line

Roll lines

CF

Zipper

Vogue pattern 2332 (current)

Issey Miyake circle skirt variations

Uneven hem takes advantage of the tendency for bias to stretch unevenly.

Square one-piece yoke with circle for waist

Skirt is one piece.

Rectangular band

Inside out: *All edges in Issey Miyake ready-to-wear are carefully finished, as in this Spring/Summer '91 Plantation twill linen suit jacket. The armhole and side seam edges were bound with bias tape.*

you need to add more, keep widening the waist by ¼-in. increments.

Don't forget to alter the waistband. The finished waistband, not including overlap for the closure, is usually 1 in. to 1½ in. smaller than the skirt waist measurement, allowing ¼ in. to ½ in. of the skirt to ease onto each quarter of the waistband.

Circle skirts tend to droop at the center front. To eliminate this, trim an additional ½ in. to ¾ in. from the front, tapering to nothing at the side seams (see nearest top drawing at left). This is most accurately done while checking the fit of the waistband; machine or hand baste the waistband in place and adjust as needed.

Because a circle skirt encompasses all possibilities of grain and bias, it has a tendency to stretch unevenly, which makes the hem crooked. This happens especially with rayons and loose or unbalanced weaves. Allowing the skirt to hang for 24 hours before hemming, as is sometimes advised, is usually inadequate; subsequent stretching may still occur. To assure an even hem on patterns that call for it, take the stretch out before you sew any seams or finish the hem. I work at the ironing board, pressing and stretching the fabric gently outward from waist to hem, holding the skirt firmly at the waist. The results may be an uneven-looking skirt edge, but you can adjust the hem at the end of construction using a hem marker.

Miyake is well aware of the tendency for a circle skirt to stretch and even takes advantage of it by designing skirts with hems that are deliberately uneven. The stretch adds to the asymmetrical nature of the skirt in a now out-of-print Vogue pattern (see the bottom left fashion sketch on the facing page). This is a marvelous skirt and is great worn sideways, with the side seams down center front and back!

Construction tips

Issey Miyake uses the sewing purist's favorite basic methods for ensuring that the inside of the garment is in keeping with the design, fabric, and integrity of the garment, yet is never overworked or fussy. When sewing Miyake patterns, be prepared to take your time and enjoy the process of fine-tuning your skills, doing beautiful work, and, yes, even fussing, and you will enjoy the surprises as you sew, fit, and finally try the garment on. Pretest techniques, seam finishes, topstitching, and stitch length.

I hand baste with abandon, using silk thread so the basting marks will not remain in the fabric, even if I press or stitch over them. Hand sewing the details is a more appropriate choice than machine topstitching for some fabrics. The look of handwovens is preserved by hand stitching the turned-under edges so that they are hidden on the inside, rather than by machine topstitching through all layers as the pattern often recommends. Hand stitching keeps the look of the edges of a silk crepe de chine blouse soft and fluid.

Make certain to transfer all markings from the pattern to fabric. I recommend using tailors' tacks in different thread colors to match and identify marking easily (see *Basics*, No. 35, pp. 18 and 20).

Always interface areas for buttons and buttonholes. There must *always* be three layers behind a button or buttonhole; the

patterns sometimes omit this detail. If the buttonholes are placed on the bias, cut the interfacing and place its grain *parallel* to the buttonhole.

The pattern instructions often say to turn edges that meet at a corner twice and stitch them, rather than finish the corner with a miter, which is what I've seen on Miyake's ready-to-wear. It is worthwhile to master mitered corners (see *Basics*, No. 35, p. 18) both by machine and by hand. Machine-stitched miters are sharp and crisp; hand-stitched miters are soft and flowing. The nature of the fabric dictates which works best. When in doubt, make a test sample.

Two common seam finishes in Miyake's ready-to-wear are French and flat-fell. Even experienced sewers will appreciate the efficient and foolproof way to do a flat-fell seam shown in No. 35, p. 54, and a great way to do a French seam is shown in No. 35, p. 18.

A French seam is perfect for straight or slightly curved seams at the shoulder, side, or for a sleeve on a dropped-shoulder garment; but for a standard set-in sleeve, a French seam is simply impossible to do well and it is inappropriate. Miyake usually solves this set-in sleeve dilemma by binding the sleeve's seam allowances with bias (see photo on facing page), or by finishing edges with serging.

Flat-fell seams work best when the seam allowances are cut a bit wider than the pattern's standard ⅝ in. Again, experiment; I prefer to start with ¾-in.- to ⅞-in.-wide seam allowances, which are called for in some Miyake patterns.

Issey Miyake uses the inset corner technique, perhaps more than any other, to set in his signature cut-with-the-front cowl

necklines and collars on blouses, jackets, dresses, and coats. (The *facing* of the jacket on the front cover also has an inset corner.) The pattern directions are not always clear, nor are they necessarily correct on this point. Patterns often have smaller-than-90° angles, which are the trickiest to sew. Careful marking, stitching, and clipping are the secrets to successful inset corners (see the drawing sequence below). Natural fibers are by far the easiest to sew and the most forgiving of small inaccuracies.

Carefully mark the seamlines using a fine chalker like a Chalkoner or thread tracing. Reinforce the inside corner seamline with slightly shorter-than-normal machine stitches and clip corner.

Pin the pieces together carefully, distributing or dividing any fullness evenly on either side of the corner pin.

Stitch the first side of the corner right up to the corner. Leave the needle down, lift the presser foot, pivot, and adjust the fullness of the fabric. Lower the presser foot and stitch the second side. ☐

Marcy Tilton is the owner of the Sewing Workshop in San Francisco, CA, and a national sewing lecturer and instructor. For a class schedule, send a double-stamped LSASE to the Sewing Workshop, 2010 Balboa St., San Francisco, CA 94121; (415) 221-SEWS. For an enlightening look at Miyake's designs from the 1980s, see Issey Miyake: Photographs by Irving Penn (Little, Brown and Company/Callaway Editions, 200 West St., Waltham, MA 02254; 1988; hardcover, $50; 96 pp.; 46 photos), a captivating collection of color and B&W photographs.

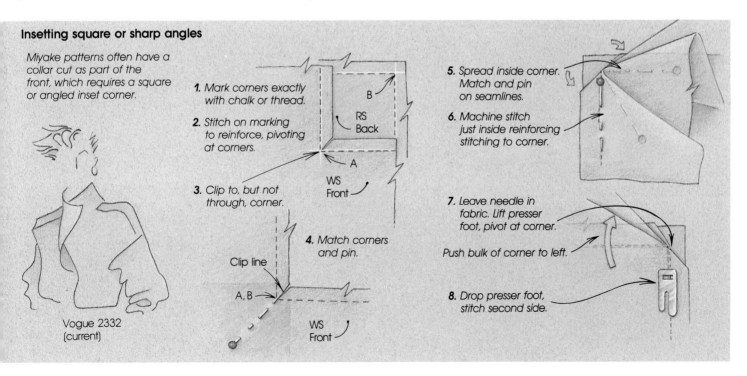

Insetting square or sharp angles

Miyake patterns often have a collar cut as part of the front, which requires a square or angled inset corner.

1. Mark corners exactly with chalk or thread.

2. Stitch on marking to reinforce, pivoting at corners.

3. Clip to, but not through, corner.

4. Match corners and pin.

B
RS Back
A
WS Front
Clip line
A, B
WS Front

5. Spread inside corner. Match and pin on seamlines.

6. Machine stitch just inside reinforcing stitching to corner.

7. Leave needle in fabric. Lift presser foot, pivot at corner.

Push bulk of corner to left.

8. Drop presser foot, stitch second side.

Vogue 2332 (current)

Lightweight wool gabardine makes an ideal unlined coat for temperate climates. Such a beautiful drape comes from keeping the sewing and finishing simple—soft fusible interfacing for cuffs, collar, and edges, and silky rayon tape binding for all the seam allowances—as described in this article. (Photo by Yvonne Taylor)

Getting the Best of Gabardine

Careful pressing, interfacing, and finishing produce a classic, long-lasting garment

by Shermane B. Fouché

*a*s a custom dressmaker, my favorite clothes are those that can go anywhere and look couture, but that don't take couture time to sew. The ideal timeless fabric for such clothing is wool gabardine. You can use the cleanest and simplest of construction and create garments that are elegantly finished.

Wool gabardine is a tightly woven twill fabric made from worsted yarns (see *Basics*, No. 41, p. 16 for weave and wool information.) The twill structure gives gabardine a beautiful drape, while the worsted character makes its surface smooth and lustrous. Gabardine doesn't soil easily because it's so tightly woven, and it resists wrinkles. The most tightly woven wool gabardines are actually water resistant.

The same qualities that make gabardine so appealing make it tricky to use. Sewers often complain that seams won't iron flat or that gabardine is difficult to interface and to topstitch. But it doesn't take fancy equipment to press gabardine, as I'll explain. And if you apply soft fusible interfacings, rather than sew-in ones, you can achieve a beautiful garment in minimal time. Here are the methods for handling gabardine that have worked for me:

Choosing a gabardine
Wool is not the only fiber made into a gabardine, but I think it has the best qualities. Rayons, cottons, and microfibers are also made into gabardines, but they don't have the same abrasion resistance, all-weather characteristic, and drape as the wools.

To test for quality, durability, and drape, I feel the fabric. I roll a length off the bolt and hold it to my waist, gather it with my hands, and let it drape over my knees to see how it falls and moves. Think about how you want your garment to look and choose the fabric accordingly.

Look for closely woven gabardines that have a high thread count per inch; I hold fabric up to the light to test for opaqueness, an indication of a tight weave. Tightly woven gabardines will be more durable, will shrink less in preparation, and will resist wrinkles more than loosely woven ones.

I've used English, Italian, and American wool gabardines. The English menswear gabardines, which tend to have a high thread count per inch, are my first choice. When crumpled in your hand and released, English gabardines have few or no wrinkles. They tend to be high priced ($40 to $60 per yard), but they are well worth the investment. When using the most tightly woven gabardines, like many of the English ones, there's no need to line them.

My next favorite gabardines are the Italians, which are usually finer and thinner. They drape beautifully with a '40s quality reminiscent of the slacks Katharine Hepburn wore, but they generally wrinkle more easily than the English gabs; they are best made into lined garments. Italian gabardines cost about the same as English ones.

There are some fine domestic gabardines, as well, and their prices tend to be lower than English or Italian ones. Their durability and drape are good, but the color range is limited compared to English or Italian gabardines, whose rich colors are so odd and wonderful.

Speaking of colors to wear, here's my suggestion: Whether you're going to make a trenchcoat, a pair of pants, or a baggy shirt, look for a color that complements your eye color. Wear that color, and you will always look fabulous.

Matching weights to garments
Generally, gabardine's character is well-suited to a tailored garment with clean, simple lines and no intricate detail. Pleats, darts, and plackets with topstitching are lovely details. Since gabardine is difficult to ease, use designs which have long, flowing lines and gentle curves, such as raglan sleeve coats and pleated slacks and trousers.

Gabardines come in light, medium, and heavy weights. Lightweight gabardine is good for full, loose, men's-style shirts with deep armholes, flat sleeve caps with little or no ease, and a one-piece collar. Full, pleated, drapey trousers (photo on p. 57), skirts with edgestitched pleats, and circle skirts hemmed to mid-calf also look great in lightweight gabardine. The raglan sleeve coat shown on the facing page required about 5 yds. of fabric, yet it is light, warm, and durable in lightweight gabardine.

Medium-weight gabardines work well for casual jackets, straight skirts, trim trousers, and shawl-collared coats with

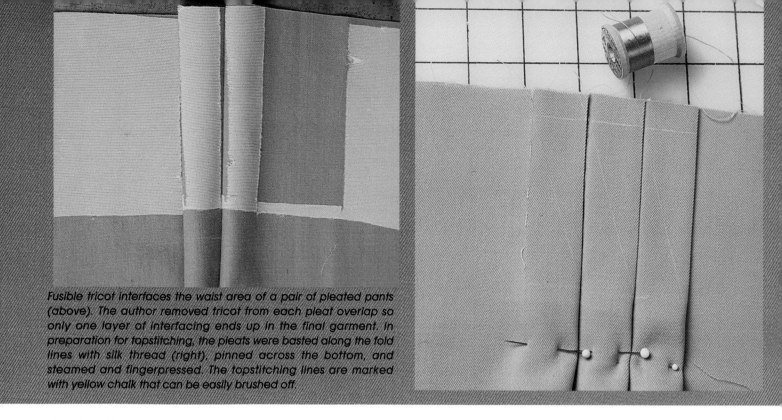

Fusible tricot interfaces the waist area of a pair of pleated pants (above). The author removed tricot from each pleat overlap so only one layer of interfacing ends up in the final garment. In preparation for topstitching, the pleats were basted along the fold lines with silk thread (right), pinned across the bottom, and steamed and fingerpressed. The topstitching lines are marked with yellow chalk that can be easily brushed off.

slim lines. Heavyweight gabardines make wonderful overcoats, outerwear in general, and hiking or riding pants.

Handwashing and preshrinking

An appealing characteristic of gabardine is that if you preshrink the fabric before construction, you can handwash unlined garments made from it, such as pants and shirts. I've found that pants with hair canvas interfacing in the waistband can be handwashed if the hair canvas was also shrunk before use. Garments that have fusible interfacings or attached linings must be dry cleaned. If you plan to have your garment dry cleaned, then simply send the yardage to the cleaners and request that they dry-clean, steam, and press it. This will ensure maximum shrinkage before the cloth is cut.

Here's the method I use to preshrink gabardine: I suggest you work with no more than three yards at a time since the wet fabric is so heavy. Half fill a bathtub with cold water and add two capfuls of a lingerie-washing liquid or high-quality hair shampoo that doesn't contain detergent or alcohol. (Alcohol acts like a solvent and will lift the color from your fabric.) Shampoos are meant to clean protein fibers, which is what wool is made up of.

Immerse the fabric, squeeze and swoosh water through it thoroughly for five to ten minutes (taking a rest every little while), then drain the tub. With the fabric still in the tub, half fill the tub once again with cold water, but don't add shampoo. Squeeze and swoosh water

through the fabric for several minutes, drain the tub, and repeat the rinse.

To dry the fabric, fold it in half lengthwise and drape it on a rod set over the tub so the water drains directly into the tub. I have a rod set perpendicular to the curtain rod, with one end resting on the wall molding. Let the fabric drain overnight. Do not twist or wring the yardage, as this could set creases. The weight of the water draining out of your fabric will relax most of the wrinkles. Let the fabric dry thoroughly, then press it, using the method described under "Perfect gabardine pressing" on pp. 56-57.

Fusibles make sewing easy

Fusible interfacing and gabardine is a marriage made in heaven. You may sew in interfacing if you prefer, but fusibles make less work.

Types of interfacing—I use only two types of fusibles with gabardine—a medium-weight weft insertion and a tricot (a knit)—alone and in combination for just the right amount of firmness. Both are synthetics; the weft insertion adds more body to gabardine than tricot. I've tried using a fusible batiste, but it's too stiff.

For outer garments such as coats and jackets, I combine weft and tricot, since two layers of weft would be too heavy, and two layers of tricot, too light. I apply weft insertion to undercollars, collar bands, pocket and sleeve welts, and in a 4-in.-wide strip down the center-front edge. The weft stabilizes the fabric. I fuse tricot to the top collar, the facings, and to

the hem facing. The tricot prevents the seam allowances in the collar and facing from showing.

Weft insertion would add too much body to a regular garment such as a shirt. I use only tricot and apply it to the cuffs, both the under and top collar, the front facing, and the front band.

For pants with a waistband, I apply weft insertion to the waistband. If I'm using lightweight gabardine and the pants don't have a waistband, I apply tricot to the body of the pants, as shown in the left photo above, and weft insertion to the facing. Bandless pants tend to roll without added body at the waist.

Non-bubble fusing—I use almost the same pressing method to apply fusible interfacing as I use for normal final pressing—a dry iron, mist of water, and a press cloth. Don't rely on a burst of steam supplied by an iron; the steam travels quickly though the porous fusible and stops short at the densely woven gabardine, causing unsightly bubbling and counteracting the fusing method. Always fuse from the garment's top to bottom with the lengthwise grain.

Working from the wrong side of the garment piece, mist the fabric lightly with a spray bottle. Lay the interfacing, glue side down, on the fabric. Mist the interfacing and pat in the moisture with your hands. Lay a press cloth over the interfacing and mist lightly. Then press and hold a hot, dry iron down on each press area for ten seconds. Do not slide the iron; that would squish the fusing agent instead of allow-

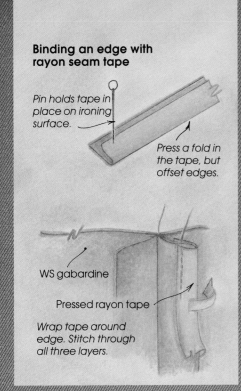

Binding an edge with rayon seam tape

Pin holds tape in place on ironing surface.

Press a fold in the tape, but offset edges.

WS gabardine

Pressed rayon tape

Wrap tape around edge. Stitch through all three layers.

A binding of colored rayon seam tape is a simple, elegant finish for seam allowance edges.

ing it to penetrate the fabric. Continue pressing and holding until you have covered the entire area to be fused. Then repeat from the right side of the fabric.

Cutting, layout, and sewing

Gabardine is easy to cut and mark. For accuracy and speed, I use pattern weights instead of pins, and a rotary cutter rather than scissors. I cut one layer of fabric at a time to get the most accurate cut possible.

Some gabardines have a nap or a sheen one way and not the other way; sometimes it's hard to see, so use the pattern instructions for nap layout. After cutting and fusing, I use tailors' tacks, a chalk pencil, and a rotary chalk dust marker (such as a Chalkoner) for marking details like pleats and darts (see right-hand photo on the facing page).

Sewing seams is straightforward. I use sizes 10 to 14 sewing machine needles and 10 to 12 stitches per inch. For most sewing, I use a size 12 needle, but a size 10 is good for single layers. I use polyester or cotton-covered polyester thread; pure cotton tends to wear and fade, and silk thread stretches too much to use for construction.

Seam finishings

Gabardine is such a beautiful fabric that I finish seams with as little fuss as possible to maintain the drape and softness.

Rayon tape seam binding—My favorite way to prevent seam allowances from raveling is to bind the edges with a folded length of plain-woven rayon seam tape

(photo and drawing above). Rayon seam tape is more flexible and softer than polyester, cotton, or self-fabric bias tape. Plain-woven tape in many different colors (select one that complements your fabric) is available by mail from tailors' suppliers such as Greenberg & Hammer, 24 W. 57th St., New York, NY 10019.

A traditional Hong Kong finish (see *Basics*, No. 41, p. 17) or pinking is also a good way to finish raw edges. I never serge gabardine edges as it tends to create a ridge on the outside of the garment when the seams are pressed. However, if you must serge, I recommend wooly nylon thread to soften the outline of the thread lines.

Topstitching—The subtle detail of topstitching, placed as near to edges as possible, makes a perfect finish.

I admit that one of the reasons I've had successful topstitching is that I use an industrial sewing machine whose presser foot pushes firmly down on the fabric. Poor topstitching—with wavy lines or puckering—is usually the result of the two layers of fabric shifting under the foot as you stitch. Here's how you can topstitch well even if you don't have an industrial machine:

Topstitching essentially presses the seams, so don't overwork the gabardine by pressing the seam beforehand. Instead, fingerpress (see instructions on p. 56), then baste the seam area with screen thread to prevent the fabric layers from shifting at all.

If you have a a straight-stitch foot (a presser foot with a small round hole), use

it for topstitching. Common on older straight-stitch machines, this foot allows the fabric layers to move less from side to side during stitching than the zigzag foot that comes with newer machines. If you find it difficult to keep your topstitching even with the seam, try a topstitching foot. This foot has a vertical plate that lines up with an edge or ridge to help keep the topstitching even.

If you are topstitching a welt seam in which both seam allowances have been turned to one side, and the allowance nearest the garment is to be trimmed, keep the allowance at least ⅜ to ¼ in. wide. Anything smaller is too narrow and will form a ridge under the fabric that will distort the topstitching.

Hand-stitched finish—Handpicking (see *Basics*, No. 41, p. 17) along the edges of a collar and front opening, instead of topstitching, is a wonderful touch for an elegant, timeless look. Gabardine has such a smooth surface that the tiny pucker of each pick shows distinctly. Handpicking can be done when the garment is finished because the stitches don't go through the back layer. It's very unusual to see handpicking on garments these days, and it will make your gabardine treasure stand out in a crowd.

Shermane Fouché is a professional dressmaker and sewing instructor in San Francisco, CA. The patterns for the coat, shirt, and pants shown in this article are available from her at PO Box 410273, San Francisco, CA, 94141.

Perfect gabardine pressing

Gabardine is such a tightly woven fabric that it resists pressing. Yet it can also be overpressed and overworked to a shine, which is difficult to remove. There are a couple of tricks I use to make sure I press just enough. If I'm pressing a seam or detail, I always prepare the fabric by manipulating the area with steam and my fingers (fingerpressing), and perhaps basting. Then, when I'm sure I'm ready to do the final pressing, I use a *dry* iron with a mist of water and a press cloth and a clapper. This way I control the amount of moisture I use, instead of relying on the steam that the iron produces, which is usually not sufficient to press such a dense fabric well.

The basic pressing equipment I use is not fancy: a treated drill press cloth (available at many fabric stores and notions mail-order companies), a plant mister spray bottle available at hardware and dime stores, and an iron. The drill cloth placed over the gabardine protects it from shine and burn. Although I have a professional Naomoto iron that can supply plenty of constant steam, I don't use the steam option for final pressing.

My wooden clapper has a point presser attached (see the left-hand photo below). I also use a length of ¾-in.-diameter wooden dowel (right-hand photo below), available from hardware stores; and a seam roll and a sleeve board, both available from sewing stores and notions mail-order companies. A point presser has a narrow, flat edge that is generally narrower than the width of two seam allowances. When you use it to press open a seam, the seam allowance edges hang off the presser surface, so they aren't pressed into the fabric. Because the seam roll and the dowel have curved surfaces, they both can be used in the same way as the point presser.

Steaming, fingerpressing, and basting—If steamed briefly, wool gabardine becomes pliable and can be gently nudged and tapped into place in preparation for final pressing. To steam, just hold a steam iron about a half inch above the fabric; don't touch the surface. While the fabric is still warm and moist, I use my fingers to press the gabardine into shape. You can fingerpress seam allowances open, position the seam along a lapel or collar edge to the underside so the line of the seam won't show after final pressing, or flatten a dart.

Sometimes I baste after fingerpressing. Pleats can be basted into position along the fold lines with silk thread, which can be pressed yet won't leave any permanent stitch impressions in the fabric.

Final pressing—To crisply press seams or fabric, I work first from the back of the fabric. Lay the garment or fabric wrong side up over the ironing board or pressing surface, and spray a light mist of water over the area. Then lay the press cloth over the misted area and mist the press cloth. With a dry iron set on high (wool setting), use a press-and-lift, press-and-lift motion on the press cloth until you have covered the entire moistened area. Don't slide the iron over the surface (this is called ironing).

If you have a stubborn area that does not flatten with the described pressing method, press the area after each press-and-lift motion with a wooden clapper, as I'm demonstrating in the left-hand photo below.

To achieve a really smooth surface in uncut yardage, turn the fabric over and repeat the pressing procedure on the gabardine's right side. Pressing

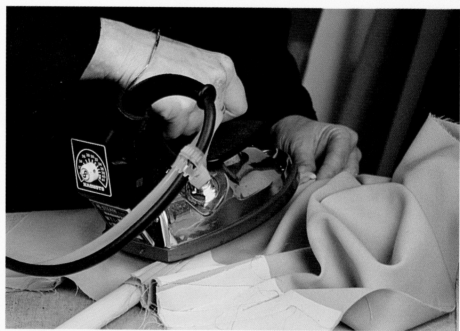

For a crisp, flat press, bear down firmly with a wooden clapper over a just-pressed area (left). The author's clapper is attached to a point presser, whose points she is using as handles. Above, an inexpensive wooden dowel makes an ideal pressing surface. Only the seam allowance gets pressed on the dowel's curve. (The press cloth normally used over the garment was removed for the photo.)

by Shermane Fouché

from the right side brings out the natural soft sheen of the lustrous wool gabardine.

Pressing seams—Gabardine needs firm pressing for crisp seams, but it's also easy to leave the impressions of seam allowance edges on the right side of the garment if you're not careful. Here's how to avoid marking the right side during final pressing.

First press with the seam allowances together to relax and set the stitches and the fabric together. Then open the allowances, fingerpress if you want, and lay the opened allowances on the point presser or seam roll. Press, using a press cloth, spray, and dry iron as recommended at left. For a very crisp press, lay the seam over the curve of a wooden dowel, as shown in the right-hand photo, facing page, and press.

Removing shine and creases—If you somehow go beyond lustrous to a flattened shine, you can remove the shine by using a steam iron. Mist the shiny area on the right side, hold your iron a half inch over the uncovered surface, and rush a burst of steam into the fabric. This should fluff the fibers and take away the shine, although you may now have to repeat the pressing procedure.

If the shine persists, you can brush the surface with short, soft brush-and-lift motions along the twill lines with a tailors' brush. This brush, available from tailors' suppliers, has outer bristles of hair and fine inner bristles of brass. It's 2½ by 3½ in. in size and is available for about $20. Shine up a scrap and test this brushing technique before you try it on your garment.

If you've put a crease where you don't want one, there's a way to remove it: Working from the back of the fabric, mist the creased area heavily, pat in the moisture evenly with a tailor's mitt (see *Basics*, No. 41, p. 18), then hold a steam iron half an inch over the moistened area and steam. This will fluff the fibers, and you can then use the pressing method described above to re-press the area flat.

Lightweight gabardine is ideal for pants and shirts. The custom touch is large running stitches along the shirt's collar and opening edges. (Photo by Susan Kahn)

Would you pass up a friendly old Harris tweed jacket simply because it was made to fit a man's broad back and shoulders? By taking the coat (above and below) apart seam by seam, you can learn a great deal about garment construction. As you carve out a custom fit (left), you may be surprised by the details you invent.

Second Time Around
Recycling a man's sport jacket for a woman's frame

by Mary Smith

did you ever wonder where old garments go when they aren't loved by anyone anymore? Sadly, many of them are forgotten and die obscurely. Happily, others are acquired by fanatics like me, who alter them to fit or take them completely apart, saving the fabric for use some other day.

Imagine the unknown treasures out there in thrift shops, Goodwill stores, your Aunt Tillie's or even Uncle Harry's closet. Gorgeous fabrics, no longer available to buy, lie hidden—already made up—just waiting for a chance to happen again.

Choosing a garment

Recycling clothing can be rewarding as well as challenging. Redoing a garment calls not only on your alteration skills but also on your knowledge of garment design.

The first thing I consider is the garment's condition. How worn is it? If it is wool, does it have moth holes? If silk, is it stressed, water-stained, or badly soiled? If it is cotton, how thin is it?

Next, I contemplate its potential. Can I use the entire garment or just parts of it? Do I want to alter it or redo it completely? At this point I make one of the hardest decisions. Am I really going to spend all the time and energy necessary to save this garment? Will I ever use the fabric elsewhere?

If I decide that altering a garment is worthwhile, I evaluate the fitting problems. If the garment is too large, I'll be eliminating fabric, a process I've become quite familiar with as I've been recycling clothing for myself since the early 1960s. Conversely, if the garment is too small, my alterations will be additions, which in many ways are more of a challenge.

Analyzing the challenge

Recently, I was asked to redo a man's Harris tweed jacket for our editor, Betsy Levine. The jacket had belonged to her father and was very beautiful.

Betsy tried on the jacket so I could determine the fitting problems we would encounter (right photos on facing page). The jacket shell did not close comfortably across the bust, and was too tight across the hips. Still, it was too large through the waist, the sleeves were too long, the sleeve caps drooped off the shoulders, and the armscyes were too deep and gaping. We would have to solve several fitting problems simultaneously as we invented design solutions to compensate for the lack of fabric.

Found garments do not offer the luxury of extra fabric, so the challenge becomes one of inventive design. The same would be true if the garment fit but was damaged in some way. At this point I spend some

From *Threads* magazine (June 1991) 35:72-76

time elsewhere going over the garment in my mind, trying to imagine designs and how to achieve them. This kind of creativity needs lots of playtime.

Taking the garment apart

When a jacket needs extensive alterations, as this one does, I take off the sleeves and begin with the shell. But first, I mark the high point of the sleeve cap with pins and check to see that the grain is straight. You will need this information later when you reset the sleeve.

When you are working on a tailored garment, especially a man's jacket, you are going to find all sorts of interlocking layers inside (photo, below left), depending on the quality of tailoring and the date of the garment. Most well-tailored jackets will have at least three layers of interfacing besides shoulder pads, wigan, and padding. (See *Threads*, No. 14, p. 42 for more on tailored jacket construction).

Carefully unpick the armscye seams, first of the lining and then of the outer fabric, leaving all padding intact for the moment. At this point you have two sleeves with lining, one shell, some loose buttons, and a lot of unanswered questions—the first of which is probably what to do next.

How to add inches

With Betsy's jacket, we decided to leave the front of the shell intact and tackle the overall problems in the back. I removed as much lining and interfacing as I could, including shoulder pads, being careful not to cut anything. While it may be difficult, it's always best not to cut excess interfacing, lin-

ing, or fabric until the end. What I couldn't remove, I let dangle.

Next I checked to see how much fabric could be let out of the side seams from an inch above the hips to the hemline. I let the hem down, opened the side seams, and found we could gain 2 in. if I restitched the seams with ¼-in. seam allowances, which I could then finish with tape as shown in the drawing on p. 60.

Since I was already working with the side seams, which are offset slightly to the back, I took the opportunity to remove the gape at the armhole back. During the pin fitting, I determined that, rather than simply removing the excess equally in both seam allowances, I should remove it from the back only, which would also reshape the seam (right drawing, p. 60).

The next option was to examine the back vent. While men's jackets have ample fabric in their lapped back vents, they don't extend much above a man's natural hipline. To determine just how much room we could gain, I removed the lining covering the vent and opened it.

It was easy to see that we could not keep the vent flapped because it would pull open, so we decided on a fancy kick pleat. The pleat would solve two problems at once: It would give us more room and also mask the fact that the jacket back at the hemline would never close completely. We decided on a thrice-folded pleat, mocking those found on men's frock coats of the 19th century. (See the drawings on pp. 61 and 62 for details). We bought a complementary fabric, a muted brown tweed, so the additions would mimic a double-woven fabric, reversed. ⇨

The first step is to separate the sleeves from the shell and inventory the innards. Most of the padding will be removed and set aside. Mary Smith begins the shell fitting at the major seams, letting out the center-back and side seams for the hips but taking them in above the waist. Even with the vent opened, extra fabric is still needed—a kick pleat is called for.

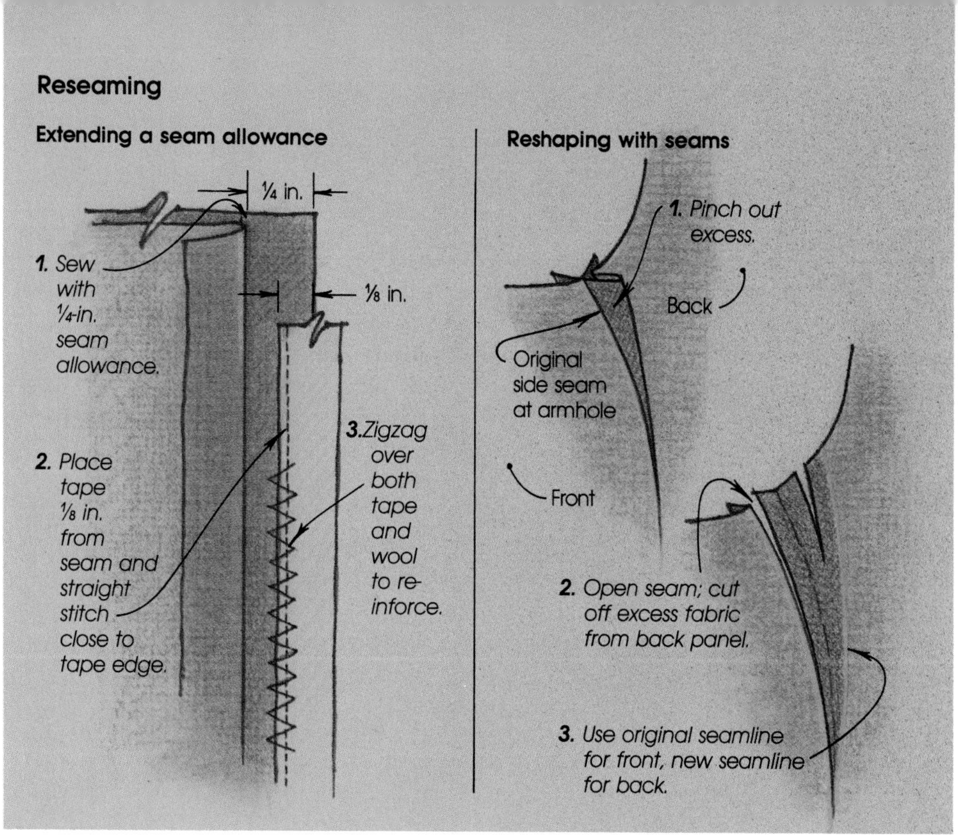
Reseaming
Extending a seam allowance
¼ in.
1. Sew with ¼-in. seam allowance.
⅛ in.
2. Place tape ⅛ in. from seam and straight stitch close to tape edge.
3. Zigzag over both tape and wool to reinforce.
Reshaping with seams
1. Pinch out excess.
Back
Original side seam at armhole
Front
2. Open seam; cut off excess fabric from back panel.
3. Use original seamline for front, new seamline for back.

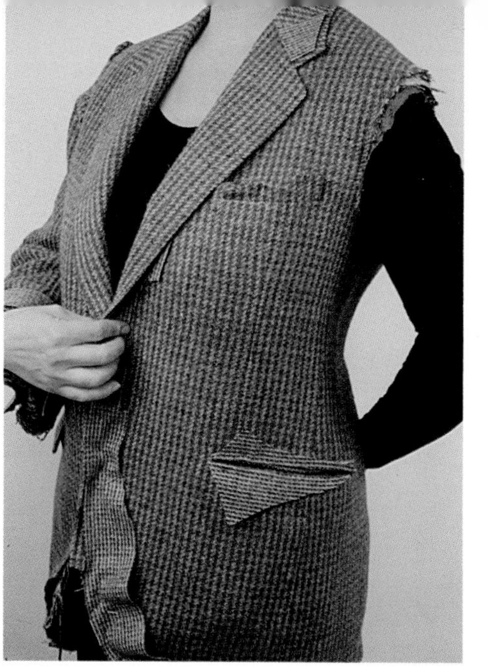

With the shoulder seam relocated, the shell is beginning to shape up. Now it's time to play with the details. Embellishments for the top collar and pockets are cut from new fabric and pinned in place. How will the sweeping curve in the fronts be edged?

Garment alignment

When doing many alterations to one garment, it is important to recheck the set of the center-back and shoulder seams on the person being fitted after making any major change. If you are fitting yourself, this can be done with a little patience. I usually pin fit the jacket at the nape of the neck, center-back waist, and hip; and by using two mirrors, I can often tell whether the center back is straight and in place. After adjusting the garment so that it hangs evenly, I check the shoulder seams. Are they straight? Are they where I want them to be for my design?

The shoulder seams on Betsy's jacket angled unattractively to the back, which created a sloping shoulder. We took in the shoulder seam from the front, changing the angle of the front seamline, which also raised the drooping waist and low armscye. Taking shoulders in is not always a simple matter of taking in the seam equally from front and back. You may have to experiment to find out which angle looks best. When resewing shoulder seams in an already-made garment, open the seam only to within ½ in. of the neckline and sew, tapering the seam to that point.

With the shoulders resewn, double-check the garment's hang. Then go ahead and sew the new side and center-back seams.

By this time you are completely launched and there is no turning back. As the photo (above) of Betsy's jacket shows, the garment has a redefined shape; it sits well and feels comfortable at the shoulders. Now the real fun begins.

Jacket front alteration

As with many endeavors, ours grew the more we worked. The changes to the back, while fine, did not make all the problems go away, nor did they entirely relieve the tightness across the chest. We checked at the front dart seams, but they had been cut open and clipped, so we couldn't use that fabric to gain inches.

To extend the front and hide the unwanted buttonholes, we turned again to our purchased fabric. I try to avoid making changes to the lapels, to preserve the detailing and hand shaping. Any changes to the front should be approached carefully. Think and design before taking any part of the lapel apart. We designed our additions by cutting scraps of fabric in a variety of shapes and pinning them to the front to discover what might be pleasing.

With Betsy's jacket, we decided to leave the hem down to gain length, recut the lower front line in a sweeping arc, and add fabric along the front edges that would taper to a ⅜-in. binding at the hemline. When changing the shape of the front, cut only the jacket front, not the facing; you'll probably need its full width to reshape later. See the drawing and photo on the facing page.

Depending on its size and shape, a front extension can be sandwiched between the front and facing, or appliquéd. Open the front lapel/facing seam only as far as necessary to accomplish the intended design. To appliqué the extension, lay the right side of the new piece against the wrong side of the jacket front and stitch together. Press and fold the fabric to the jacket right side and pin in place for final shaping.

Before completing the appliqué, turn the jacket inside out. Now is the time to shape the facing and pin it to the addition on the inside. Since we are working with a very malleable Harris tweed, some pinning, hand maneuvering, plus a wet pressing cloth will accomplish this. If your fabric is a worsted, you may have to trim as well. On the right side, pin under the seam allowance along the addition edge and put the jacket on for yet another look. I don't stitch the front facing or edges yet; there are still a few decisions to make.

Designing details

In the beginning, one of our ideas was to do something with the pockets, possibly alter the flap shape or eliminate it. Of course, now we wanted to add some of the new fabric to the collar, as well as trim and reshape the upper breast pocket, details shown on the facing page.

We went back to our cutout fabric shapes to test our ideas, and came up with the pocket design. Making patterns for top and bottom flaps is easy. Just trace around the fabric shapes you like, adding ¼-in. seam allowances when you cut. Before removing the paper patterns, use them to wrap (and press) the seam allowances around, except where they will be inserted.

Working from the outside, open the seam holding the pocket flap and remove it. Save it; you may need the fabric later. Try not to disturb the welt. To minimize the difficulty of attaching the new appliquéd "flaps," I do it entirely by hand, as shown on the facing page, center. ⇨

The jacket transformed

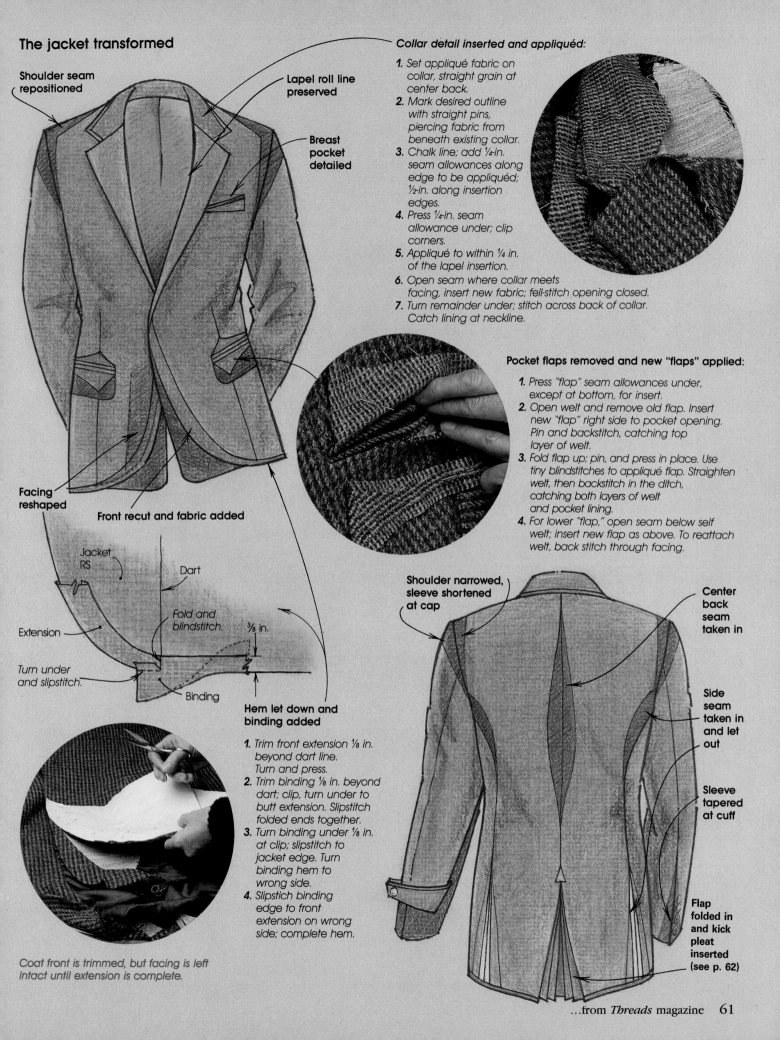

Shoulder seam repositioned

Lapel roll line preserved

Breast pocket detailed

Collar detail inserted and appliquéd:

1. Set appliqué fabric on collar, straight grain at center back.
2. Mark desired outline with straight pins, piercing fabric from beneath existing collar.
3. Chalk line; add ¼-in. seam allowances along edge to be appliquéd; ½-in. along insertion edges.
4. Press ¼-in. seam allowance under; clip corners.
5. Appliqué to within ¼ in. of the lapel insertion.
6. Open seam where collar meets facing, insert new fabric; fell-stitch opening closed.
7. Turn remainder under; stitch across back of collar. Catch lining at neckline.

Pocket flaps removed and new "flaps" applied:

1. Press "flap" seam allowances under, except at bottom, for insert.
2. Open welt and remove old flap. Insert new "flap" right side to pocket opening. Pin and backstitch, catching top layer of welt.
3. Fold flap up; pin, and press in place. Use tiny blindstitches to appliqué flap. Straighten welt, then backstitch in the ditch, catching both layers of welt and pocket lining.
4. For lower "flap," open seam below self welt; insert new flap as above. To reattach welt, back stitch through facing.

Facing reshaped

Front recut and fabric added

Jacket RS

Dart

Extension

Fold and blindstitch.

⅜ in.

Turn under and slipstitch.

Binding

Hem let down and binding added

1. Trim front extension ⅛ in. beyond dart line. Turn and press.
2. Trim binding ⅛ in. beyond dart; clip, turn under to butt extension. Slipstitch folded ends together.
3. Turn binding under ⅛ in. at clip; slipstitch to jacket edge. Turn binding hem to wrong side.
4. Slipstitch binding edge to front extension on wrong side; complete hem.

Coat front is trimmed, but facing is left intact until extension is complete.

Shoulder narrowed, sleeve shortened at cap

Center back seam taken in

Side seam taken in and let out

Sleeve tapered at cuff

Flap folded in and kick pleat inserted (see p. 62)

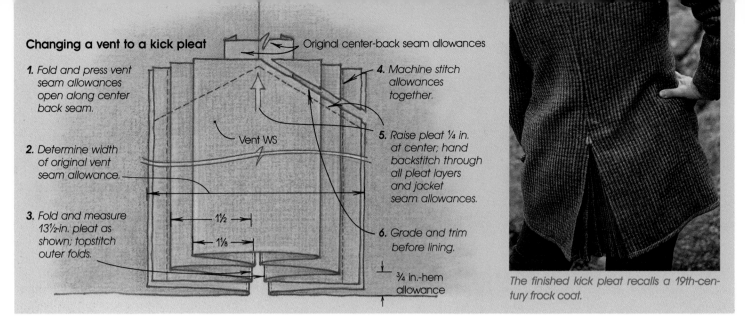

Changing a vent to a kick pleat

1. Fold and press vent seam allowances open along center back seam.

2. Determine width of original vent seam allowance.

3. Fold and measure 13½-in. pleat as shown; topstitch outer folds.

Vent WS

Original center-back seam allowances

4. Machine stitch allowances together.

5. Raise pleat ¼ in. at center; hand backstitch through all pleat layers and jacket seam allowances.

6. Grade and trim before lining.

1½

1⅛

¾ in.-hem allowance

The finished kick pleat recalls a 19th-century frock coat.

Finishing the front edges

When all the design details are in place and finished, it's time to complete the jacket front and bottom. The front extension must blend neatly into the hem binding, and the reshaped facing must be unobtrusively attached.

Edges—I wanted a fabric strip wide enough to give the garment a ³⁄₈-in. binding plus a hem inside, so I cut the strip, on straight grain, ¾ in. plus hem allowance. I attached the strip to the lower edge of the jacket, which I trimmed evenly, beginning at the end of the lower pocket dart, where the front extension ends. With right sides together, using a fraction less than ³⁄₈ in. as a seam guide, I stitched the binding to the jacket, ending at the kick-pleat seam. Now the kick-pleat seam could be finished and the two hems aligned.

Where the front extension (sewn to the jacket wrong side and pressed to the right side for a clean finish) and the binding (sewn to the right side and pressed to wrong side) meet, I trimmed both close, turned the ends under, and blindstitched to join them, as shown at left, p. 61.

Closures—The buttonholes on a man's jacket or fine custom coat are corded; removing the stitches is not difficult. Just run your seam ripper under the stitches along the cord and gently remove both. The stitches are easy to pick out. Usually this opening can be covered and hidden, but if not, you can close it with fusible interfacing. To be sure the fusible will hold, ravel a few strands of wool and do a fake reweaving, if you're really fussy.

I placed an eyelet buttonhole on each side of the jacket so the fronts would come together much as a French cuff does when secured with two engaging buttons toggled together. This is one of those design deci-

sions prompted by the need to gain inches.

At this point I blindstitched the reshaped facing to the folded edge of the binding and the front extension. Except for the fine tailoring to finish the inside, the jacket shell is ready to receive sleeves.

Attaching the sleeves

Do you like your sleeves the way they are, and merely want to reset them? Or are they long, loose, and sloppy? Is the cuff opening too wide? You may set the sleeves and then tackle the cuffs, or rework the sleeves before setting them. For ease of fitting, I prefer to set the sleeve and then redo the cuffs, even though the jacket bulk can be cumbersome. Remove the sleeve lining, and if you are going to redo the cuffs, let them down now.

Align the high point of the sleeves with the new shoulder line and pin the sleeve to the jacket to see just what has happened since altering the shell.

Because I had closed the armhole enough to raise it, now of course the sleeve cap was too big. Raising the sleeve reduces the circumference and shortens it. Just how much to trim from the cap and where to position the sleeve/shoulder seam is a matter of trial and error. I usually pin and baste until I like the line and the fit. If you are going to reuse the shoulder pads, or any of the padding, insert them at this time. When you like the shape, fit, and hang of the sleeve in the armhole, carefully mark the seamline position on both with chalk or thread basting.

I usually find that there is more than enough fabric for seam allowances of ½ in. to ⅝ in. At this point I trim the shoulder line and sleeves and reset them, reinserting the shoulder pads and padding and tacking them in place.

To complete the theme of the French-cuff closure, the sleeves will have turned-

up cuffs. Most jackets of this quality have ample sleeve hems, so your design options aren't limited.

Lining and fine tailoring

Now is the time to cut and trim all those dangling interfacings, linings, and other bits you've been working around. I usually sit where it is quiet, with several pairs of scissors, some needles, pins, and thread. I trim all the seam allowances that will be hidden by linings. Those that will remain exposed, I finish off in the style of the original.

I had thought I would cut away most of the front interfacing for a soft Armani look, but since I handled and reshaped the fronts so much, the interfacing had to go back in place. For stability, I tacked the interfacing the full length of the jacket front. The front lining no longer reached the side seam, but I decided a full back lining was called for anyway. Adding new lining is easy. Cut a new piece wide enough to reach the front lining plus two seam allowances and long enough to match the front lining. Sew lining addition to back lining and then sew lining side seams. Reattach the lining along the facing down to the hem, as well as at the shoulders with a running stitch. Make sure the lining covers the pads and padding along the armhole. Reattach the lining to the hem.

Most sleeve linings are done by hand. The lining will probably need some changes to fit; in some cases excess fabric can be pleated as ease. Most tailors use tiny overcasting stitches all around the armhole, incorporating ease as they go. At the cuff, measure the lining to the end of the sleeve, adding 1-in. ease, adjusting as needed. All that's left to do is to attach the buttons. □

Mary Smith is associate art director of Threads. She is contemplating, for her next time around, a black tuxedo with tails recently bought at Goodwill.

Jacket Lining Made Easy

Sew and insert it completely by machine

by Cecelia Podolak

From *Threads* magazine (February 1992) 39:62-64

the fastest and easiest way to line a tailored jacket is by bagging. In this technique, borrowed from the garment industry, the lining is entirely sewn to the jacket by machine and the garment is turned right side out through the sleeve, back vent, hem, or center-back seam. The name results from the bag or sack that forms as you work through the process. A few minor revisions to the lining pattern for additional ease make the lining fit into the jacket just as if it had been carefully positioned and hand sewn.

Lining fabrics

The primary function of a lining is to conceal inner construction details, but linings also help make jackets more wearable. Jackets will slide on and off more easily, will wrinkle less, and the outer fabric will wear better in a lined jacket.

Linings need not be strictly utilitarian and can add a splash of color or pattern to the jacket. Current fashion shows us jacket sleeves rolled up to display contrasting or coordinating lining fabrics. Piping inserted around the inner edge of the jacket facing, as shown in the photo at left, makes an especially elegant finish.

My favorite lining fabrics are crepe-finished rayon or lightweight blends of rayon and acetate. These fibers are comfortable to wear because both rayon and acetate allow the body to breathe. I avoid the lighter colors of lining because they don't conceal inner jacket details (interfacing, pockets, seams) well.

Acetate twills, jacquards, or plain-weave fabrics in medium weight cover details and are comfortable to wear. Acetate satins, especially those which have been backed with an interlining fabric for extra warmth, are heavier and are really better for lining coats.

Don't rule out blouse and dress fabrics, especially if you want a print or patterned lining. Do remember, though, that polyester does not allow the body to breathe and can be uncomfortable in jackets. Rayon, unless blended with polyester, will wrinkle and may not be as slippery as you'd like a lining to be. If you want the ultimate in luxury, treat yourself to silk lining: charmeuse, satin-backed crepe, or even one of the new

The hallmark of a tailored jacket is an impeccable lining (left). You can insert linings by machine and still achieve impressive results—a little like having your cake and eating it, too. (Photo by Susan Kahn)

sueded silks might be more expensive and less hard wearing than regular lining fabrics, but should last for the life of the jacket.

Making a lining pattern

If the jacket pattern you're using doesn't include a lining pattern, cutting one from the jacket pattern is a simple matter. The basic rule is to remove the facing width from the pattern pieces and then extend this new line an additional 1¼ in. for seam allowance, as shown below.

A back-neck facing is essential for the bagging technique and you will need to design one if there is none included with the pattern. Trace around the jacket back pattern piece following the neckline curve, shoulder seam, and center back and making the width 3 to 3½ in., or equal to that of the front facing at the shoulder. Retain seam allowances at the shoulder and make the grainline parallel to the center back. Place this piece on a fold of fabric when cutting.

Add a pleat to a jacket with no center-back seam by placing the center-back line of the lining pattern ¾ in. to 1 in. from the fabric fold when cutting. This pleat extends from neck to hem. For a pattern that has a center-back seam, add 1 in. for the neckline pleat, continue cutting parallel to the seam to within 1 to 2 in. above the waist, then taper quickly to the regular ⅝-in. seam at the waistline.

Cut the underarm of the sleeve and the body ½ in. to ⅝ in. higher than the jacket pattern from notch to notch, as shown in the drawing at right. When you trim the jacket seam allowance in the underarm, it will stand upright rather than being pressed flat. Making the lining larger here will eliminate binding under the arm and keep the lining from distorting the jacket fabric.

Shoulder pad allowance can be removed as shown in the drawing at right. If you choose not to adjust the lining, you'll simply end up with more ease.

Extend the jacket and sleeve lining hems ½ in. beyond the finished hem length on the jacket pieces. When the lining is sewn in, the excess length will form a jump hem or small ease pleat. Press this toward the hem.

The grainline for the lining pieces will be the same as on the jacket pattern. You can cut sleeve and pocket linings on the bias for greater flexibility.

Modifying a lining pattern

Many patterns contain separate pattern pieces for a lining, or have lining cutting lines marked on the jacket pieces. When a lining pattern is provided, compare the underarm height of the body and sleeve pieces with the garment pieces. If they are the same, modify the lining pieces for bagging by raising the underarm as previously described.

If there is no back-neck facing, make a pattern for one as explained. Remove the width of the facing, less a ⅝-in. seam allowance, from the lining pattern.

Check the hem depth used for the fashion fabric of both the jacket body and sleeves. You will need at least a standard 1½ in. to allow the lining to be sewn to the jacket. Add to your pattern if less is allowed. Make sure the bottom and sleeve hems are cut ½ in. longer than the finished hem.

Cutting and sewing the lining

Using a rotary cutter and mat will definitely speed up the process of cutting slippery lining fabrics. Pin only the grainlines of the pattern pieces and use weights to hold the corners in place. A metal-edged ruler will keep the tissue pattern from creeping and will ensure straight lines. Mark any darts or tucks with a tracing wheel and dressmakers' carbon paper.

Assemble the lining on either a regular sewing machine or on a serger, pressing the seam allowances open or to one side. Press the darts in the opposite direction of the jacket darts to eliminate bulk. Sew the center-back seam, and if there's a pleat, machine baste it closed on the center-back line. Usually, 1 in. at the waist and 1½ in. at the neck and hem are held together with regular machine stitching instead of basting.

I prefer to turn the jacket through the sleeve seam, so I leave one sleeve underarm seam open for 10 to 12 in. about 1½ in. below the armhole. To keep the lining from fraying during handling, I serge or zigzag the raw edges of the opening. Ease the sleeve caps and machine stitch them in place, then press the seam allowances toward the sleeve cap.

Staystitch and clip the front and back lining necklines to allow easier joining to the jacket neck facings. ⇨

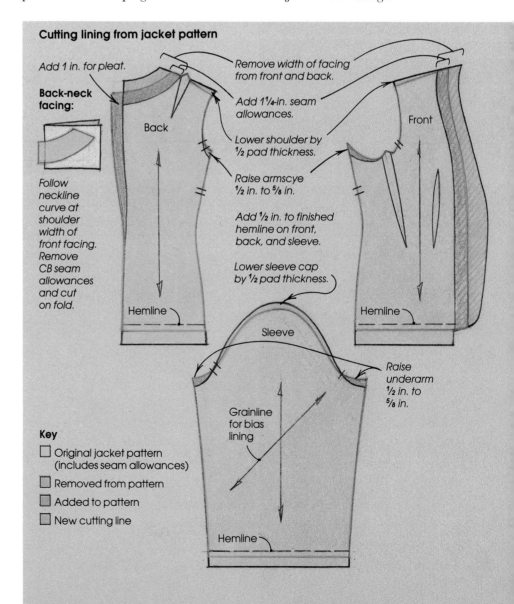

Cutting lining from jacket pattern

Add 1 in. for pleat.

Back-neck facing:

Follow neckline curve at shoulder width of front facing. Remove CB seam allowances and cut on fold.

Back

Hemline

Remove width of facing from front and back.

Add 1¼-in. seam allowances.

Lower shoulder by ½ pad thickness.

Raise armscye ½ in. to ⅝ in.

Add ½ in. to finished hemline on front, back, and sleeve.

Lower sleeve cap by ½ pad thickness.

Front

Hemline

Sleeve

Grainline for bias lining

Raise underarm ½ in. to ⅝ in.

Hemline

Key

☐ Original jacket pattern (includes seam allowances)

☐ Removed from pattern

☐ Added to pattern

☐ New cutting line

Bagging the lining

Finish the jacket completely and press it before attaching the lining (see the article on pp. 28-33 for construction methods). Tack the shoulder pads in place and complete the backs of any bound buttonholes. Finish the lower 3 in. of the inner edges of the front facing on the serger or overcast them by hand, but don't tack them in place at this point. Catch-stitch both the jacket and sleeve hems in the *middle* of the hem allowance.

If you're adding piping to the lining, sew it to the inner edge of front and back facings. The piping stitching should be on the ⅝-in. seamline, with the raw edges of the piping in the seam allowance. If you want to make your own piping, fold 1¾-in.-wide bias strips of a matching or contrasting fabric over a soft, small-diameter wool yarn. Stitch close to the yarn with a zipper foot. The raw edges of this piping will be even with the raw edges of the facing when you stitch. Pin the piping to the right side of the facing beginning and ending at the finished hem of the jacket. Begin and end the stitching about ¾ in. below the top edge of the hem facing as shown in the top inset drawing below. Use a zipper foot to attach the piping so the stitching will be as close to the yarn as possible. Now you're ready to sew the lining to the jacket.

Facings—With the jacket wrong side out, match the lining to the entire front and back facing as shown in the top drawing below, and pin it in place with right sides together. Fold the lining hem up at the front facing edge so the raw edge of the lining hem is even with the raw edge of the jacket hem. If you've used piping, fold the loose end up and over the lining.

Stitch the lining to the facing with a ⅝-in. seam allowance. Use a zipper foot, if needed, to retrace the piping stitching. Set the stitching by pressing with an iron before turning. Turn the jacket right side out, pushing the sleeve lining into the sleeves, and press the lining seam away from the front edge (toward the side seam), smoothing the seam allowance between the lining and the facing. Press carefully, keeping the iron from flattening the piping.

Sleeves—Pin each underarm sleeve seam through all thicknesses about 6 in. above the hem so that the lining sleeve will not twist in the jacket. To machine stitch the lining and sleeve hems together, reach into the open sleeve seam and across the back between the lining and jacket. Grasp the two hem allowances with right sides together, and pull the entire pinned unit through the opening as shown in the lower drawing below. Carefully pin the circle of fabric and lining right sides together, matching the underarm seams and easing the jacket fabric where necessary. Machine stitch with a ⅝-in. seam allowance. Set the stitching with the iron. Pull the sleeve back through the open seam allowance where it will now be right side out. The lining will form a jump hem above the cuff; carefully press this pleat in place. Remove the pin. Repeat for the second sleeve hem.

Jacket hem—For a final time, reach into the open sleeve seam and pull out the hems of the jacket body and lining, keeping the right sides together. Pin, matching side seams and easing fabric to the lining where necessary. Machine stitch using a ⅝-in. seam allowance starting and ending as close to the front facings as possible. Set the stitching with the iron before pushing the jacket back through the sleeve opening so it is right side out. The lining will form a jump hem which you will press into place.

Finishing—Close the open sleeve seam, with wrong sides together and seam allowances folded to the inside. Edgestitch through all layers close to the folds (see *Basics*, No. 39, p. 16). The tiny ridge that this produces will be invisible from the right side of the garment.

Carefully position and match the lining to the armhole of the jacket, keeping the armscye seam allowances of lining and jacket aligned all the way around. Working from the right side of the jacket, stitch in the ditch for ½ in. along the jacket side seam near the armhole to hold the lining in place.

The final step is to secure the lower edges of the front facing by fusing or hand catch-stitching. □

Cecelia Podolak wrote about contemporary jacket tailoring methods in Threads *No. 37. She is a Clothing Specialist with the University of British Columbia.*

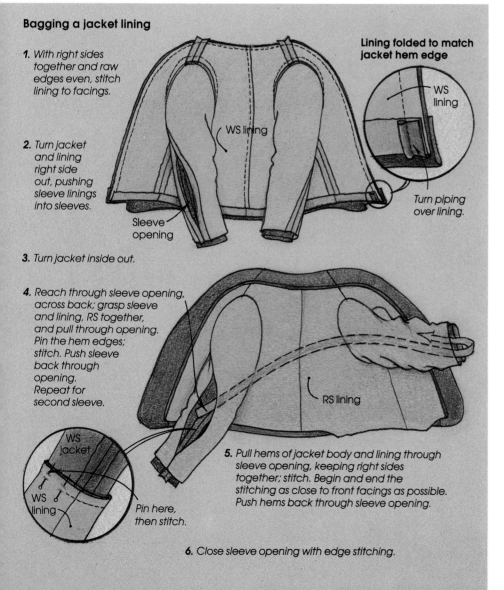

Bagging a jacket lining

1. With right sides together and raw edges even, stitch lining to facings.

2. Turn jacket and lining right side out, pushing sleeve linings into sleeves.

Sleeve opening

WS lining

3. Turn jacket inside out.

4. Reach through sleeve opening, across back; grasp sleeve and lining, RS together, and pull through opening. Pin the hem edges; stitch. Push sleeve back through opening. Repeat for second sleeve.

WS jacket

WS lining

Pin here, then stitch.

Lining folded to match jacket hem edge

WS lining

Turn piping over lining.

RS lining

5. Pull hems of jacket body and lining through sleeve opening, keeping right sides together; stitch. Begin and end the stitching as close to front facings as possible. Push hems back through sleeve opening.

6. Close sleeve opening with edge stitching.

Designed for Living, Not for Fashion

American designer Bonnie Cashin defined the '60s' functional minimalism

by Mary Elliott

A gridded pattern and sewing instructions for Cashin's Noh coat at left appear on pages 72-75.

how many modern designers are there whose garments you could positively identify, at a glance, without first seeing the label? I'd have to say "Not many," and I'm a costume historian. Among American designers, however, there's one whose clothing is undeniably and irrefutably recognizable. Bonnie Cashin carved her name in fashion history with one truly innovative and incredibly focused collection after another, from 1952 to well into the 1970s.

Bonnie Cashin's signature style is responsible for so many contemporary design concepts it's hard to tally them. Perhaps her most enduring contribution is the idea of "layering" clothing to produce a combination of style and comfort. But she also brought to fashion hardware closures, leather bindings, the poncho, the parabola cut, the Noh coat, the bubble coat, canvas outerwear, and the combination of hand-loomed English and Irish wools with leather, jersey, and cashmere. At the same time her construction methods were classic examples of elegant simplicity, easily within the reach of any careful sewer. On the following pages, I'll examine the cut and construction of some characteristic Cashin garments and accessories from the collection at Mount Mary College (in Milwaukee, Wisconsin), like those shown here, but first let's backtrack a bit and discover the source of all this inspiration.

From Hollywood to Seventh Avenue

Bonnie Cashin is a native Californian whose family provided the perfect environment for a fledgling designer. Her mother was a custom dressmaker with shops in San Francisco and Los Angeles. Her father was a photographer, painter, and inventor. This combination may well have helped Cashin develop what she considers essential for a designer—"a sense of wonderment."

Armed with strong sewing skills and that "wonderment," she started work at a Seventh Avenue sportswear house, but soon thereafter, in 1943, returned to California to take a motion picture contract offered her by Twentieth Century Fox. During her seven years in Hollywood she designed costumes for 60 films, including *Laura* and *Anna and the King of Siam*. I found it most interest-

Clean lines, functional details, and the best fabrics and leathers assembled into streamlined, layered outfits; these were the hallmarks of Bonnie Cashin's decade-defining garments. From left to right: the kimono-cut Noh coat, leather knickers with leather-bound jersey top and knit leggings; and the parabola skirt. (Photo opposite by Yvonne Taylor)

ing, even a bit odd, that after so much theatrical experience, her fashion designs bear little or no trace of Hollywood glitter. "I always felt that [at Fox] I wasn't a designer *per se* but an assistant to the author," Bonnie told me in an interview in January 1990 (all the quotes herein are from that interview). "I remember a picture that had nothing glamorous in it—*A Tree Grows In Brooklyn*—and I met the author, Betty Smith, much later.

"We had lunch and she said, 'I just want to tell you, young lady, that every character looked exactly as I imagined them.' I thought that was the most marvelous compliment I've ever had."

In 1949 Cashin returned to New York, and by 1952, she had established her own design house, which lasted until the late 1970s. During those years Bonnie Cashin rewrote the book on American sportswear and established a new look for the contemporary woman.

No useless seams

The first thing that strikes you about "Cashins" is their simplicity and cleanliness of form. There's not a ruffle, tuck, bead, or flounce to be found on these clothes. They are totally uncontrived and modern in appearance. It is no coincidence that Bonnie refers to "carving" silhouettes out of fabric rather than to draping material. She has always emphasized "...the graphic quality of shapes *sans* torturing fabric with useless seams and darting... It's much easier to design a fancy style than a simple one, but I try to avoid it because, when it comes to wearing it, you really don't want things that are fussy. All our lives are too complicated to put up with that sort of thing in clothes."

A perfect example of her graphic simplicity also became one of Bonnie's most famous silhouettes; her "parabola" designs, like the skirt shown on p. 67, whose pattern is above, are based upon a mathematical figure often seen in graphs. Skirts, coats, and jackets rise high in front and gently taper to a longer back. The black leather skirt is lined with plushy grey wool, and was shown with a black knit turtleneck, grey cashmere leggings, and boots. I think it looks more contemporary than most current sportswear, yet it was introduced 21 years ago!

The pink cape with matching hood shown on the facing page exemplifies the utility of Bonnie's architectural form. Designed for

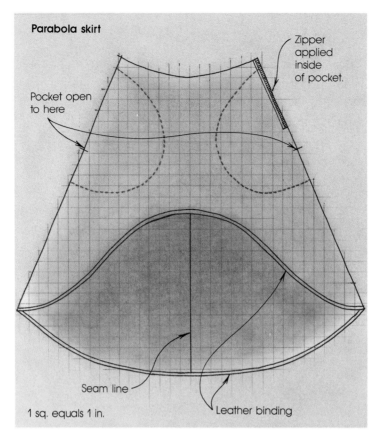

Parabola skirt

Pocket open to here

Zipper applied inside of pocket.

Seam line

1 sq. equals 1 in.

Leather binding

truly nasty weather, the hood (see pattern at right) completely covers head, neck, and shoulders, and the cape itself is double-layered and has no arm slots. The center front closes only at the neck, so the wearer doesn't feel trapped, and the pockets can be accessed from inside or out, as shown in the drawings at right, and described below.

Today's "ethnic" fashions usually emphasize the decorative surfaces and intense colors of traditional garments. Bonnie Cashin saw straight through the surface to the pure lines and simple, no-shoulder-seams cut of timeless garments like the poncho and the kimono. Her Noh coat and variations on it like the one shown on p. 66 and on pp. 72-75, cut on kimono-like lines, became a recurrent theme and a favorite of travelers throughout the world. Roomy and cut in a variety of lengths, it was made in mohair, tweed, leather, suede, and canvas in endless color and texture combinations. The poncho, another favorite of Bonnie Cashin's because it could double as a lap robe when travelling, was used in every collection and every combination as a layering tool.

Textures and contrasts

A gorgeous fabric bound and trimmed in a perfectly-matched leather is characteristic of Bonnie Cashin's designs. Luxurious mohairs, alpacas, hand-loomed tweeds in sumptuous color combinations, buttery kid suedes, rib knits, and jerseys, set off by the ever-present leathers, are a visual feast for

the eyes and a sensuous delight to the hand. Where did she find these incredible textiles?

It all started with what Cashin calls a "barnstorming trip" to Ireland. She bought a very heavy Irish tweed, only 28 in. wide, and started playing with it. It had what she referred to as "shape and character—some hunting and a chance encounter led me to two or three other small mills that proved a delight to work with. Not only would they let me combine funny colors, or enlarge a plaid to giant size, but they'd suggest I only order 20 yards to try!" Experimentation with colors and yarns followed ("They did question me when I asked for a 32 oz. fabric, like carpeting!") until decisions for specific collections were made. Cashin's manufacturer responded by dyeing all of his leathers and suedes to match or coordinate, until their leather library included some 80 shades. The resulting fabrics are among the most beautiful ever used by an American designer.

Construction

Sewing with such lush, thick fabrics calls for innovative construction methods. Cashin's garment are, of course, entirely machine made and mass produced, but she devised original finishes and new techniques that whisper "top-quality," despite their obvious simplicity.

Linings—Linings, at least traditional ones, are noticeably absent here. The interiors of coats, suits, and dresses are beautifully finished either with untraditional linings (like the parabola skirt's wool plush or the rain cape's self-lining) or most often, with no linings at all. Cashin explains her reasoning: "I couldn't bear the usual crepe and satin linings, feeling they had no textural affinity with the fabrics I liked. First of all, matching was a problem, and then cleaning was a problem. Aesthetically the linings were offensive (unless they were jersey, alpaca, or fur) and they simply defeated a beautiful cloth. I'd rather have a handsome fabric go it on its own."

Unlined garments naturally demand that more be attention paid to inside details, and Cashin's don't disappoint. The inside seams are treated to flat-felled seams, sometimes as wide as ³⁄₄ in. to accommodate the thick fabrics, and to complementary leather bindings. Hemlines are no

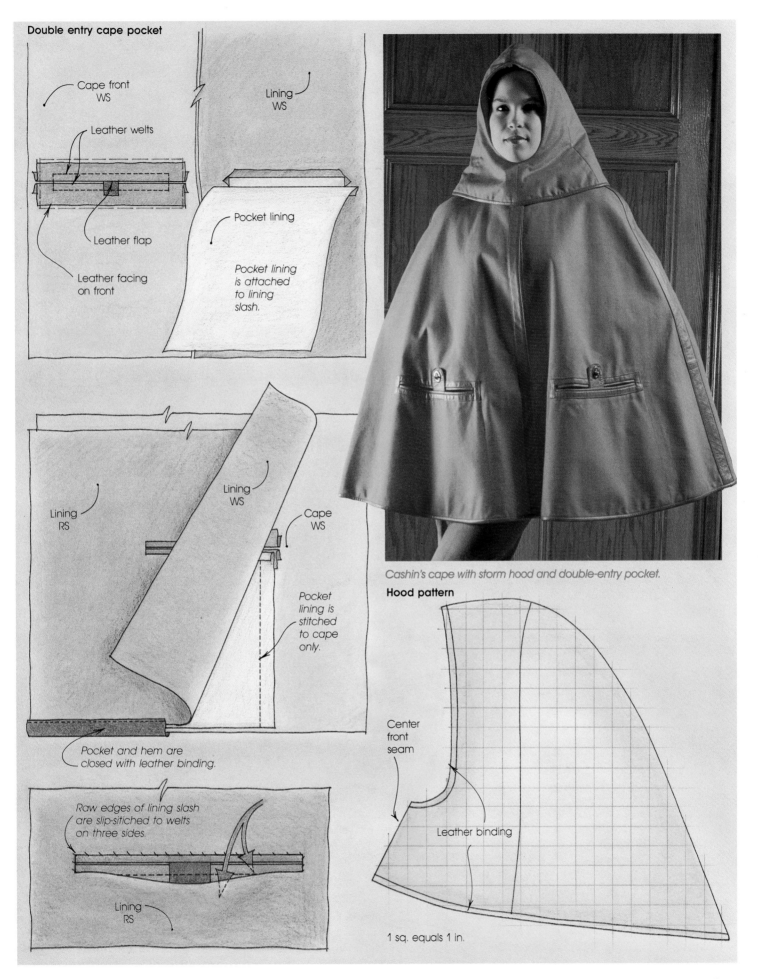

Double entry cape pocket

Cape front
WS

Lining
WS

Leather welts

Leather flap

Leather facing
on front

Pocket lining

*Pocket lining
is attached
to lining
slash.*

Lining
RS

Lining
WS

Cape
WS

*Pocket
lining is
stitched
to cape
only.*

*Pocket and hem are
closed with leather binding.*

*Raw edges of lining slash
are slip-stitched to welts
on three sides.*

Lining
RS

Cashin's cape with storm hood and double-entry pocket.

Hood pattern

Center
front
seam

Leather binding

1 sq. equals 1 in.

Cashin's unlined interiors required beautiful but simple seam finishes, like the Noh coat's leather-bound seam, above right, which matches the finish on all the garment edges, and also the finish of the patch pocket mouth. A typical Cashin patch pocket is sewn to the inside of the garment, raw edges folded under, so the stitching line forms a shape on the garment surface. Inseam pockets can also be leather-bound, like the one above left, even if otherwise constructed normally, with a tweed facing and a light-weight pocketing. At far right, Bonnie Cashin in her studio, dressed in her working uniform of tights and a turtleneck.

problem because in almost every case they too are bound in leather.

Pockets—Cashin's pocket solutions are masterful. A favorite idea is to apply a patch pocket to the wrong side of the garment, so the resulting stitching line becomes an integral part of the exterior design. The patch's seam allowances are turned under, or if the garment is lined, like the parabola skirt, the patch is sandwiched under the lining; no raw edges ever show. The patch pocket on the plaid Noh coat variation, shown above, is applied to a simple leather-bound flap, which is all there is to the coat front; Cashin simply bound the patch opening to match, and positioned it a little inside the flap.

Another bound opening is shown in the same photo; in this case, Cashin bound both sides of a traditional in-seam pocket with leather to match the leather hem binding and waistband. The pocket opening is faced with tweed, but the pocketing is made of a lightweight synthetic.

The lining for the double-entry pocket Cashin concocted for her blazing pink cape hangs from the cape lining; both are cut from the canvas outer cloth. As shown in the drawing on p. 69, Cashin made a slash through both layers, then applied a leather double-welt pocket to the top layer, with a leather facing on the outside. To the lining slash she

stitched the top edge of the pocket patch, which folds down from the slash to the bound hem. She stitched both sides of the patch to the front layer to create the pocket; the raw edges of the lining layer were folded under and slipstitched to the leather welt strips.

Engineered for living

It is important to note that all of the pieces in a Cashin collection were designed not to stand alone but to be part of an entire concept of dressing. Coats went on top of sleeveless vests—went on top of skirts, pants or knickers—went on top of cowl neck sweaters—went on top of body suits and leggings. Bonnie Cashin borrowed from the Chinese idea of judging appropriate dress by whether it was a "one-shirt day or a seven-shirt day." Comfortable dress the Cashin way is the ability to add or subtract components to create one's own personal environment. "If fashion design thinking is healthy, it relates to the larger environment. Fashion can enrich that environment, not only by pleasing the aesthetic eye, but by freeing the contemporary female to get on with her own involvement in a very challenging, interesting world."

This ability to add or subtract layers never resulted in a bulky appearance. When *Sports Illustrated* presented her with their Designer of the Year award (in 1958 and again in 1963) they referred to "...a fully or-

ganized Cashin traveler looking as efficiently engineered as a jet airplane."

The engineered appearance of Cashin clothing carried through to closures as well. Instead of the traditional buttons and zippers, Bonnie used turn screws, toggles, dog leash hardware, even ski boot closures. She told me, "I got the turn-screw idea because I owned a convertible when I first started working in Hollywood. You had to fasten down the top, and I thought those were cute little gadgets!" These most unusual devices meshed perfectly with her concept of form, function, and economy of line in design.

Bonnie Cashin describes her approach best herself: "You can make fashion out of anything, even a gunny sack. You can publicize it, get the word around—all of that. Even no clothes becomes fashion, as in *The Emperor's New Clothes*. But it has nothing to do with design. Design has to be for living—the natural outcome of a stream of consciousness. The real endangered species of our time is the artist/designer. What motivates my work is love: love of color, love of texture, line and form, love of rearranging elements in response to patterns of living. And, love in the doing." □

Mary Elliot is curator of Historic Costume at Mount Mary College, Milwaukee, WI. She wrote about Norman Norell in Threads #25.

Binding with leather, real or fake

By Mary Elliott

I've experimented with some scraps of Cashin's original fabrics and leathers and found that with a little basting I could get good results when binding a substantial fabric like a tweed or bouclé. The drawings at right show how I duplicated Cashin's signature ¼-in. binding.

I used a #11 leather (wedge-point) needle, setting my stitch length to about 7 per in. (3.5 metric). My iron was set to wool with no steam, and I found that pressing over ordinary brown paper worked fine to keep the leather from buckling. As long as the leather strips were uniform thickness, I had no problem folding them evenly over to the wrong side; I basted them in place with an ordinary heavy needle. When I did the final stitching from the right side, the leather was too thick to allow me to get exactly on top of the earlier seam, but I examined Cashin's seams and they were always a little away from the first seam, too. A final press with brown paper made a big difference in the finished appearance.

Using synthetic leathers— I also tried binding with UltraSuede, Facile (which is the lightweight version of UltraSuede), and UltraLeather (see Sources at right). My results with these new manmades were marvelous. UltraLeather created beautiful, uniform bindings on the thickest Cashin tweeds I had. It was so pliable that I could narrow the binding width to ³⁄₁₆-in. without a problem, impossible (at least for me) with real leather. Because it has a knit backing and stretches easily I was able to manipulate it around corners with no difficulty.

UltraSuede and Facile worked equally well. I found Facile ideal for binding wool jersey because it's so lightweight. I had to staystitch the edge seam carefully, but after that it was a breeze.

Ronda Chaney, a sewer with lots of UltraSuede experience, has these suggestions for handling synthetic leathers: For binding strips, cut them on the crossgrain, the direction of greatest stretch. Rotary cutters with new blades are the best choice for accurate strip cutting; if you prefer scissors, use your sharpest ones.

Treat the fakes like knits, using a size 75/11 stretch needle, like a Schmetz HS, and sew with a long staple poly thread, like Mettler or Gutermann. Set your machine for 10 to 12 stitches per inch (2 to 2.5 on a metric machine) when you're making seams, and 6 to 8 per inch (3.5 to 4 metric) for topstitching, and test liberally on scraps for the best tension and pressure settings. A walking foot is a great help with these fabrics, particularly if they drag, which can increase the stitch density enough to perforate the fabric. Roller feet can help, but walking feet work best. If you don't have either, try pulling the fabric taut as it feeds, with equal pressure in front of and behind the needle.

Contrary to rumor, it's definitely possible to pin into the fakes, and to rip seams. If you're careful to use new needles and sharp pins, and the settings above, the holes will close within 24 hours. UltraLeather is less forgiving, so try a smaller machine needle, like a 60/8 or 65/9. Use long glass-headed pins and test them to see if they slip in easily. Change needles as soon as the stitches seem less than perfect, or every

five hours. For hand basting, use the smallest leather needles you can find, and the same poly threads you're sewing with.

You can press the fakes, and fuse to them; use a wool setting. EasyKnit is a good choice for stabilizing strips and trims, and you can position the strips securely at edges with ⅛-in. strips of fusible web. Cover your ironing board with a thick terry towel, and always keep the napped side of the suedes next to the pile. To fuse, dampen and wring out a construction press cloth, and layer this over the fusible against the wrong side of the fake; use the same pressure you would to fuse an ordinary fabric. For the final press of a binding strip, sandwich the strip between layers of towel, if it's sueded.

Sources for leather, real and fake

Real leather
Any leather from Tandy or other dealers that's called garment leather, and most leathers under 2½ oz., can be sewn on ordinary machines and will work for bindings.

Tandy Leather Co.
Box 2934, Dept TH,
Fort Worth, TX 76113
Tandy offers a variety of smooth and sueded garment leathers. Send $2 (refundable) for Tandy's 100-page mail-order catalog.

Synthetics and Notions

Mary Jo's Cloth Store Inc.
401 Cox Rd.
Gastonia, NC 28054
(800) MARY-JOS (627-9567)
All colors of UltraSuede and Facile, some UltraLeather, good prices, no minimum order.

G-Street Fabrics
11854 Rockville Pike
Rockville, MD 20852
(800) 333-9191
Most colors of all three fakes, including 12 colors UltraLeather; minimum order ⅛-yd.

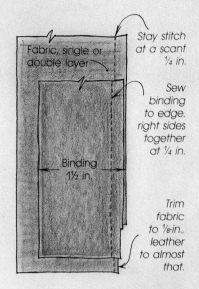

Fabric, single or double layer

Binding 1½ in.

Stay stitch at a scant ¼ in.

Sew binding to edge, right sides together at ¼ in.

Trim fabric to ⅛-in., leather to almost that.

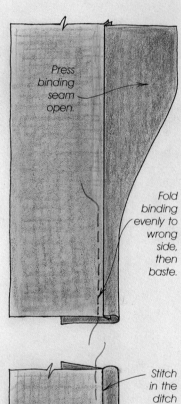

Press binding seam open.

Fold binding evenly to wrong side, then baste.

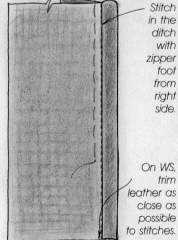

Stitch in the ditch with zipper foot from right side.

On WS, trim leather as close as possible to stitches.

Sewing Instructions for Cashin Coat

Fabrics: Wool tweed, bouclé, melton, wool double-cloth, hand-loomed mohair. Not suitable for obvious diagonals.

Yardage: 2⅔ yds. 56-in. to 60-in. wide fashion fabric. ⅓ yd. lightweight pocket lining. 7½ yds. leather or suede binding (1½ in. wide); add 1¼ yds. if binding interior underarm seam. If you're binding with synthetic leather or suede, ⅓ yd. of 45-in. fabric is plenty, assuming you cut the strips 1½ in. wide on the cross grain.

A note on sizing

The Cashin coat is remarkably adaptable to a wide range of sizes, probably because there are no precise fitting points, like shoulder seams, cuffs, or a waistline. The coat is 46⅜ in. long in front and 44½ in. in back, 50 in. around at the underarm, and 56 in. from sleeve hem to sleeve hem. It looks great on anyone from a 5 ft. 10 in. size 18 to a 5 ft. 4 in. size 8. Body and sleeve length are the only feasible places to alter the garment, if necessary. To alter the length, slash and spread (or overlap) front and back equally on horizontal lines anywhere below the side seam opening, then redraw the side seams so they're straight lines again. Adjust the pocket opening edge to match the new side seam angle. To alter the sleeve length, simply add or subtract at the sleeve hem; the limiting factor is of course the width of your fabric.

Step 1: For each pocket, place pocket lining over pocket piece, wrong side of pocket to right side of lining. (This assumes that you will want the wrong side of the finished pocket to match the wrong side on the interior of the coat.) Stitch together along curved edges. Trim seams to ⅛ in., press open, and turn lining to inside. Press flat. This step encases the raw edges inside the pocket.

Step 2: To bind pocket mouth, slash seam allowance of pocket and lining to circles and trim away allowances at opening. Baste raw edge of lining to raw edge of pocket along entire straight edge. Apply leather binding to pocket mouth, catching lining too: Staystitch the raw edge at a scant ¼ in., then stitch binding to edge at ¼ in., face down to pocket side (more details on p. 71). Fold binding over edge, baste, then stitch in the ditch from the pocket side to secure, and trim close to stitching. Tuck the raw edges at each end of binding strips under and tack, as shown in the drawing below.

Step 3: Position pockets on inside of coat along placement lines indicated on pattern. Baste into position. The raw edges on either side of the bound openings will be caught when leather binding or other edge finishing is applied to coat edges.

Step 4: Topstitch pockets to coat, stitching through all thicknesses ¼ in. from pocket edges. This stitching will show on the front of the coat, so if you are working with a fabric that will not camouflage the stitching, be very careful to make the stitching lines smooth and precise. One method is to make a cardboard template from the topstitching guide, and use it to trace the guide exactly onto the coat front, then topstitch pocket from the coat side.

Step 5: Fold fabric at shoulder point (point G) right sides together, and stitch each underarm seam starting at slash on side seam, pivoting at circle and matching notches on sleeve seams. Slash to circle after seam is sewn.

Step 6: On the Cashin coat this interior underarm seam allowance is bound with leather. If you want this type of finish, do it now. Stitch the binding strip to the seam allowance before you trim and grade the seam, then fold binding over and stitch in the ditch to secure. An alternative method is to use a flat-felled seam.

Step 7: Bind all seams (center front, side seams to slash, hem, and sleeve hems) in leather as described in Step 2, or use an alternate finish. If using leather strips seamed together, position a seam at neckline center back and work outwards from there.

Step 8: On the Cashin coat a small piece of leather is used at the interior junction of the side seam slash and underarm seam to cover the three binding junctions, as shown in the drawing at right. Machine or hand-stitch in place, with underarm seam binding folded to the back.

Finishing Binding Edges

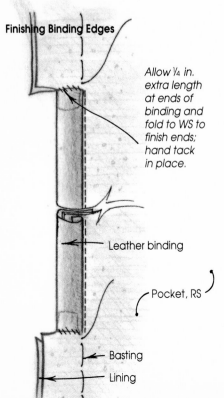

Allow ¼ in. extra length at ends of binding and fold to WS to finish ends; hand tack in place.

Leather binding

Pocket, RS

Basting

Lining

Underarm Binding Finish

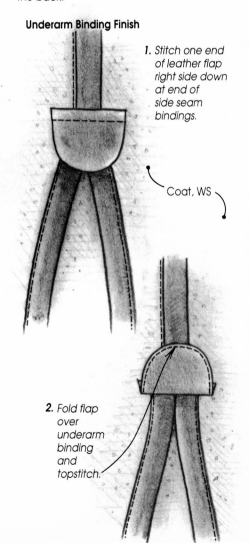

1. Stitch one end of leather flap right side down at end of side seam bindings.

Coat, WS

2. Fold flap over underarm binding and topstitch.

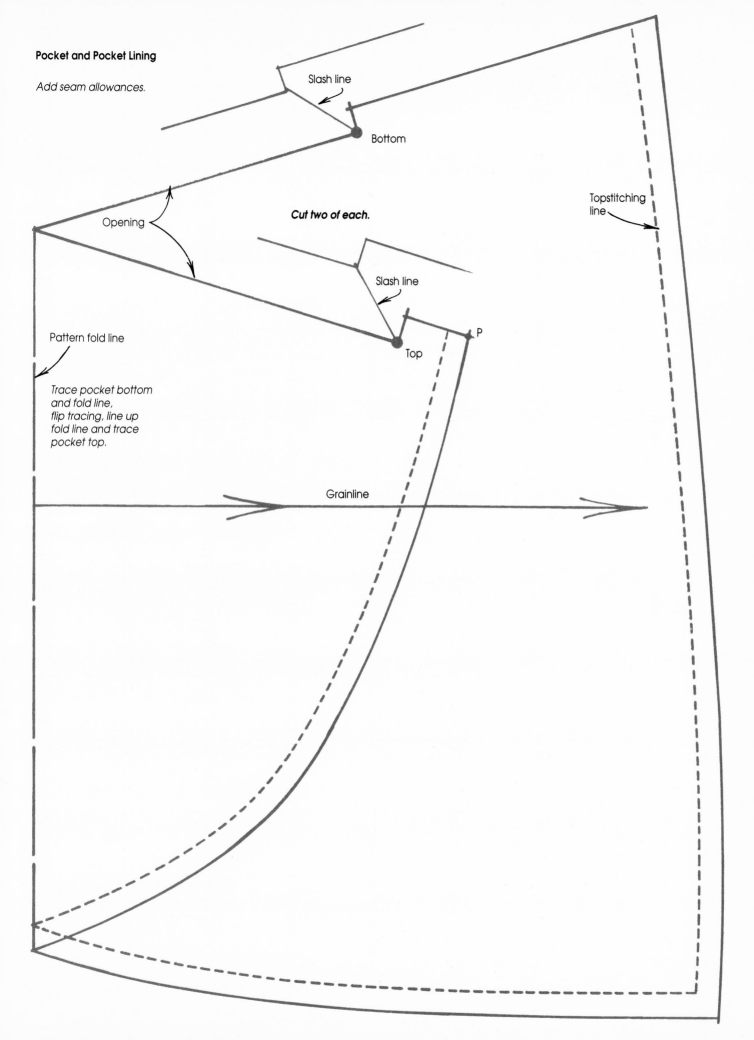

Pocket and Pocket Lining

Add seam allowances.

Slash line

Bottom

Opening

Cut two of each.

Slash line

Top

P

Pattern fold line

*Trace pocket bottom
and fold line,
flip tracing, line up
fold line and trace
pocket top.*

Topstitching
line

Grainline

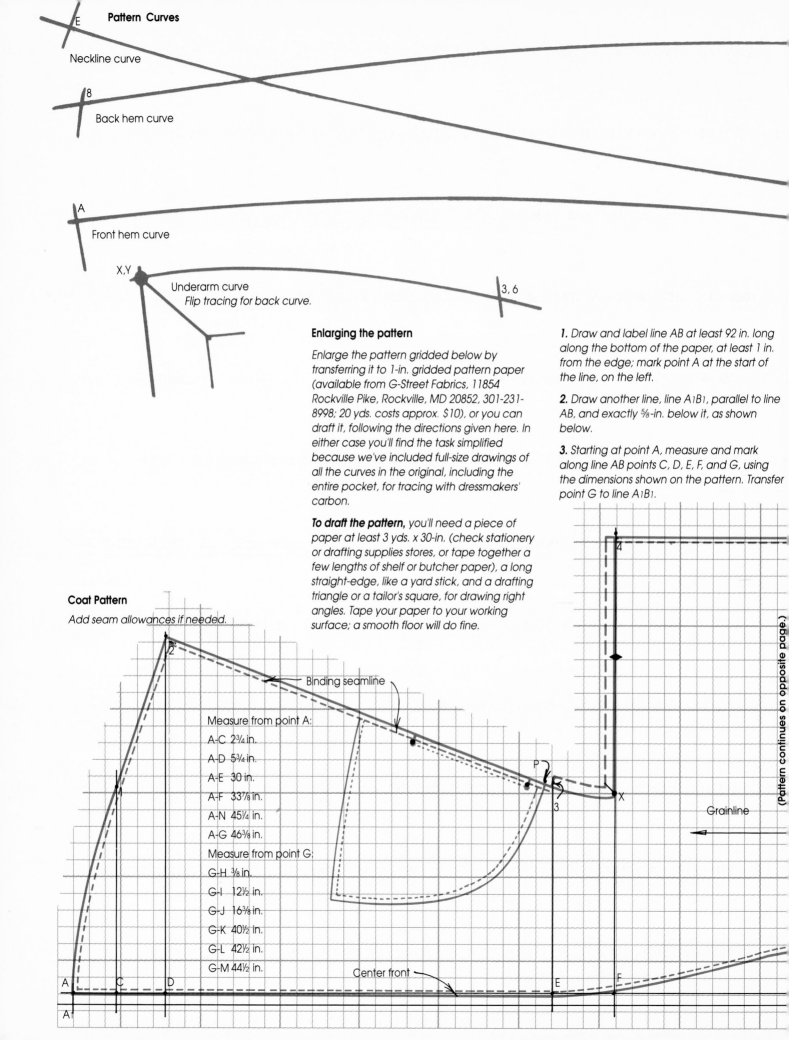

Pattern Curves

E

Neckline curve

8

Back hem curve

A

Front hem curve

X,Y

Underarm curve
Flip tracing for back curve.

3, 6

Enlarging the pattern

Enlarge the pattern gridded below by transferring it to 1-in. gridded pattern paper (available from G-Street Fabrics, 11854 Rockville Pike, Rockville, MD 20852, 301-231-8998; 20 yds. costs approx. $10), or you can draft it, following the directions given here. In either case you'll find the task simplified because we've included full-size drawings of all the curves in the original, including the entire pocket, for tracing with dressmakers' carbon.

To draft the pattern, *you'll need a piece of paper at least 3 yds. x 30-in. (check stationery or drafting supplies stores, or tape together a few lengths of shelf or butcher paper), a long straight-edge, like a yard stick, and a drafting triangle or a tailor's square, for drawing right angles. Tape your paper to your working surface; a smooth floor will do fine.*

1. Draw and label line AB at least 92 in. long along the bottom of the paper, at least 1 in. from the edge; mark point A at the start of the line, on the left.

2. Draw another line, line A₁B₁, parallel to line AB, and exactly ⅝-in. below it, as shown below.

3. Starting at point A, measure and mark along line AB points C, D, E, F, and G, using the dimensions shown on the pattern. Transfer point G to line A₁B₁.

4

X

Grainline

(Pattern continues on opposite page.)

Coat Pattern

Add seam allowances if needed.

2

Binding seamline

P

3

Measure from point A:

A-C 2¾ in.

A-D 5¾ in.

A-E 30 in.

A-F 33⅞ in.

A-N 45¼ in.

A-G 46⅜ in.

Measure from point G:

G-H ⅜ in.

G-I 12½ in.

G-J 16⅜ in.

G-K 40½ in.

G-L 42½ in.

G-M 44½ in.

Center front

A   C   D

A₁

E   F

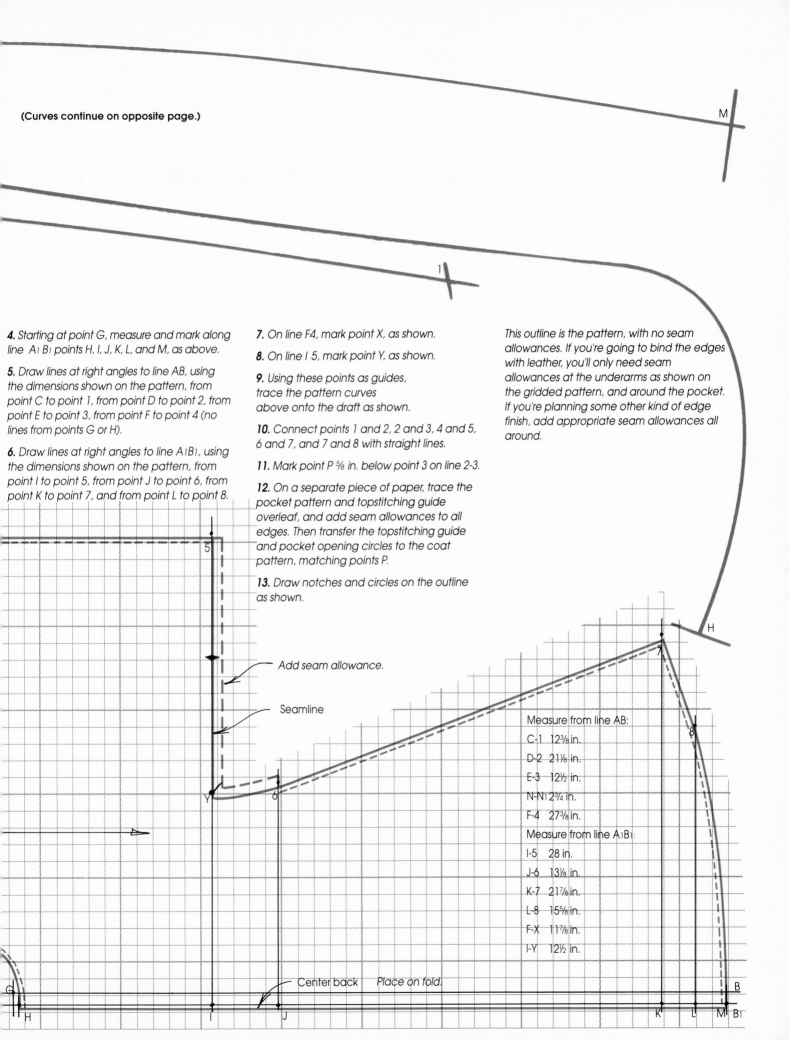

(Curves continue on opposite page.)

M

1

4. *Starting at point G, measure and mark along line A₁ B₁ points H, I, J, K, L, and M, as above.*

5. *Draw lines at right angles to line AB, using the dimensions shown on the pattern, from point C to point 1, from point D to point 2, from point E to point 3, from point F to point 4 (no lines from points G or H).*

6. *Draw lines at right angles to line A₁B₁, using the dimensions shown on the pattern, from point I to point 5, from point J to point 6, from point K to point 7, and from point L to point 8.*

7. *On line F4, mark point X, as shown.*

8. *On line I 5, mark point Y, as shown.*

9. *Using these points as guides, trace the pattern curves above onto the draft as shown.*

10. *Connect points 1 and 2, 2 and 3, 4 and 5, 6 and 7, and 7 and 8 with straight lines.*

11. *Mark point P ⅝ in. below point 3 on line 2-3.*

12. *On a separate piece of paper, trace the pocket pattern and topstitching guide overleaf, and add seam allowances to all edges. Then transfer the topstitching guide and pocket opening circles to the coat pattern, matching points P.*

13. *Draw notches and circles on the outline as shown.*

This outline is the pattern, with no seam allowances. If you're going to bind the edges with leather, you'll only need seam allowances at the underarms as shown on the gridded pattern, and around the pocket. If you're planning some other kind of edge finish, add appropriate seam allowances all around.

5

Add seam allowance.

Seamline

Y   6

H

7

8

Measure from line AB:

C-1   12⅜ in.
D-2   21⅛ in.
E-3   12½ in.
N-N1 2¾ in.
F-4   27⅜ in.

Measure from line A₁B₁:

I-5   28 in.
J-6   13⅛ in.
K-7   21⅞ in.
L-8   15⅝ in.
F-X   11⅞ in.
I-Y   12½ in.

Center back   *Place on fold.*

G

H

I   J   K   L   M B₁

B

Convertible collar has two roll lines so it will fall properly when coat is worn open or buttoned to the neck. See instructions for interfacing on p. 81.

Simplified interfacing pads hollow of shoulder and strengthens coat front edges for durable wear. See instructions on p. 79.

A half lining requires careful finishing and layering of lining over facing, facing over pocket.

Pocket cover of coat fabric hides pocket. See instructions on p. 78.

Underlap of vent is lined. See instructions on p. 80.

Techniques for a Topcoat

Men's wear tailoring tips for a long-lasting, unisex garment

by David Page Coffin

Scouting about for my next sewing project last winter, I conceived the desire for a wool topcoat. I'd once had a perfect one. Made from a heavy Donegal tweed full of multicolor flecks, with raglan sleeves, leather buttons, welt pockets, and a collar that looked great flipped up to cover my neck, it had cost $20 at a thrift shop. Equal to the fiercest winters, it was finally done in by a summer in a damp basement.

I'd seen coats like it on both men and women, cloaking them in an atmosphere of a British mystery; images of foggy heaths and chilly London train stations followed in their wakes. I checked the exclusive department store whose label my old coat had carried; the current version was available only in a nondescript gray, had hardly any swagger, and cost more than $700. I looked through the pattern books and all the tailoring books I had; no men's patterns, a few women's patterns that came close, and no description of proper overcoat construction.

I noticed that many women at work had overcoats similar to the one I had in mind, and I examined them carefully; the ready-to-wear tailored men's version, as I remembered, was made with better materials and a great deal more hand work. Finally, at a vintage clothing store, I found the perfect specimen (far left coat in the photo on the facing page). The details were right, the construction was

A topcoat is an ideal introduction to hand tailoring, as author David Page Coffin discovered when he made the brown tweed copy of the light green coat at far left. Customize a coat you make from a commercial pattern with any or all of his finishing details. (Photo by Susan Kahn)

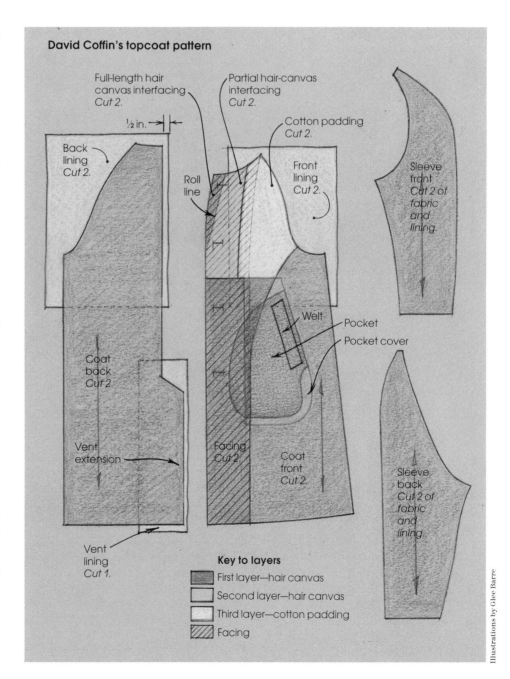

David Coffin's topcoat pattern

Full-length hair canvas interfacing *Cut 2.*

Partial hair-canvas interfacing *Cut 2.*

Cotton padding *Cut 2.*

½ in.

Back lining *Cut 2.*

Roll line

Front lining *Cut 2.*

Sleeve front *Cut 2 of fabric and lining.*

Welt

Pocket

Pocket cover

Coat back *Cut 2.*

Facing *Cut 2.*

Coat front *Cut 2.*

Sleeve back *Cut 2 of fabric and lining.*

Vent extension

Vent lining *Cut 1.*

Key to layers

▨	First layer—hair canvas
☐	Second layer—hair canvas
☐	Third layer—cotton padding
▨	Facing

Illustrations by Glee Barre

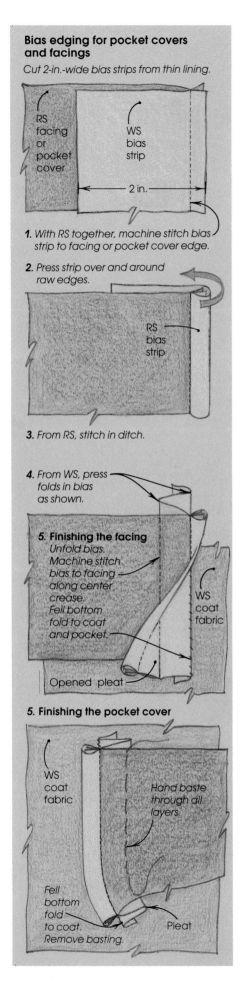

Bias edging for pocket covers and facings

Cut 2-in.-wide bias strips from thin lining.

RS facing or pocket cover

WS bias strip

2 in.

1. With RS together, machine stitch bias strip to facing or pocket cover edge.

2. Press strip over and around raw edges.

RS bias strip

3. From RS, stitch in ditch.

4. From WS, press folds in bias as shown.

5. Finishing the facing
Unfold bias. Machine stitch bias to facing along center crease. Fell bottom fold to coat and pocket.

WS coat fabric

Opened pleat

5. Finishing the pocket cover

WS coat fabric

Hand baste through all layers.

Fell bottom fold to coat. Remove basting.

Pleat

first-rate, and it fit. Years ago I would have been content simply to wear it, but now I wanted to unravel its mysteries and make a copy for myself.

First I called custom tailor Stanley Hostek in Seattle, WA; yes, he'd made topcoats and would be happy to look at my prototype and give me some advice. Following his directions, and those in a basic tailoring text, I completed a coat (right coat in photo on p. 76) that is nearly an exact copy of the vintage original. It completely fills the bill: When I wear it I feel just like Lord Peter Whimsey.

Easing into tailoring

An overcoat is a perfect introduction to working with traditional tailoring techniques on traditional materials. The fit of an overcoat, with straight sides and very little shaping, is uncritical compared to more closely fitting garments, such as a jacket, especially if the overcoat has raglan sleeves. The thick wool is the most forgiving of fabrics to sew and press. The collar holds none of the terrors of a collar/lapel combination. My coat has a hair-canvas interfacing to keep the front edges sturdy and stable, but the interfacing layering is much less complex than that for a suit jacket. There's no interfacing at all in the back.

Even the best men's topcoats have only a half lining, to allow you to reach your pants through the double-entry welt pockets. The heavy cotton chamois pockets, which are normally hidden from view by a full lining, are concealed by a coat-fabric pocket cover held fast to the coat by a bias strip of lining. Likewise, the front facings, from the hem of the half lining down, are finished with bias strips, which are felled to the pocket and the coat. The back vent is finished with a lining on the underlap.

Most interesting to me is the coat collar, which has two roll lines built into the undercollar: one for when the coat is buttoned to the neck, the other for when the coat is left unbuttoned.

Commercial coat patterns—The basic sleeve and body shapes are all you need from any of the following patterns to make a coat in the way I describe. You can apply a few or all of the techniques below to a commercial coat pattern. Look for a pattern that has a center-back seam, two-piece raglan sleeves, a button-to-the-neck collar, and separate facings rather than facings cut in one with the coat fronts. Use the general cut of my coat, shown on p. 77, to determine how to cut and position the interfacing, lining, and pocket covers.

Although the patterns are all women's with one exception, they all come in sizes large enough to equal a man's size 40 or larger; just read the bust size as chest size and make the buttonholes on the left. All the patterns call for shoulder pads, so there should be plenty of room for a man's shoulders without pads.

I suggest you make a muslin version to be sure you like the silhouette, to see if you want to redraw the neckline for the collar, and to determine the precise position of the pocket openings and the coat hem. The shoulder seams could also be adjusted to eliminate shoulder pads.

Patterns that have a button-to-the-neck collar are probably easier to use than ones that have a classic jacket lapel/collar combination with a defined roll line; Vogue's 2530 (Calvin Klein) and Style 1191, a double-breasted trenchcoat (narrow the fronts so they have only a 2-in. lap at the center front) both fit the bill. Style 1624 has the right collar and raglan sleeves, but it has much more flare than my coat; recut the pattern for straighter sides. New Look 6021, Vogue 1614, and Butterick 6735 have a lapel/collar neckline; if you want to button them to the neck, you'll have to add a button and raise the neckline.

Must reading—Perhaps the most essential piece of equipment I had was a tailoring text; most texts will get you through the basic steps, such as adding the collar, pad stitching, and making hand-stitched buttonholes. I used my text (see below) along with the original coat to figure out every step and its proper sequence in the construction. Only those details that aren't explained in a standard text are covered in detail here.

My text of choice is *Classic Tailoring Techniques: A Construction Guide for Men's Wear* and the companion text for women's wear, both by Robert Cabrera and Patricia Meyers (Fairchild Publications, 7 West 34th St., New York, NY 10001; women's text, 1989; men's text 1984; both hardcover, $25 each). I used mainly the men's wear version, but I think the women's wear book is more interesting. Most of the basic material on jacket construction and fitting is duplicated in each book, but the women's version covers a lot of unusual subjects like making unlined jackets, lined and pleated pants, curved piped pockets, and tailored mandarin collars.

Fabrics and interfacings—The main materials you need for a coat are heavy 100% wool fabric, hair canvas and cotton padding for the coat front interfacing,

French linen for the collar interfacing, and both heavy- and regular-weight lining fabric (rayon will wear best) for the half lining and for binding the pocket and facing edges. All the interfacings are available from tailoring suppliers (see Sources, on p. 81).

I used a subtly patterned tweed, but the coat can be made from any heavy coating. The advantages of tweed are many: Its grain is easy to see because the weave is so visible, and it's easy to hide hand stitches in the textured fabric. I discovered that the pattern helped me keep my hand stitches regular by providing guidelines: I could take a stitch at every recurrence of a particular thread. Solid-color and smooth coatings are also easy to stitch into invisibly, but the details, like topstitching and pocket welts, show up more clearly.

The interfacing requires two layers of nonstretchy hair canvas (called hymo) and a third layer of cotton padding. The collar is interfaced with French linen, which will stretch and shape with pressing. You'll need 4 yds. of hymo and ½ yd. each of linen and cotton padding. About 4 yds. of ¼-in.-wide cotton twill tape is sufficient for stabilizing the front and armscye edges.

The coat's half lining requires about 1½ yds. of 45-in.-wide heavy lining, such as a flannel-backed rayon, for the body, sleeves, and back vent. Also get 1 yd. of regular-weight lining for the bias strips.

Threads and needles—Tailors use silk for all their sewing because it's the strongest and most flexible of natural-fiber threads. Silk is what I used; you can substitute a 100% cotton or polyester, but silk is easy to find at tailors' suppliers. I used size A for the hand and machine sewing, and size F (buttonhole weight) for the hand-stitched buttonholes. A ½-oz. spool of each was plenty. I matched the darkest color in my fabric (black), and also used a little matching brown size A silk for hand sewing the lining in place.

For all machine stitching, I used a size 100 needle so the stitches wouldn't skip when piercing the thick layers of fabric. For hand sewing, between needles in sizes 7 through 10 worked well. I ran every length of hand-sewing thread, except for the basting thread, over a lump of beeswax before sewing to prevent kinks or snarls.

Construction steps

I recommend you read through the construction details that follow to get a feel for the steps you'd like to use. I've sum-

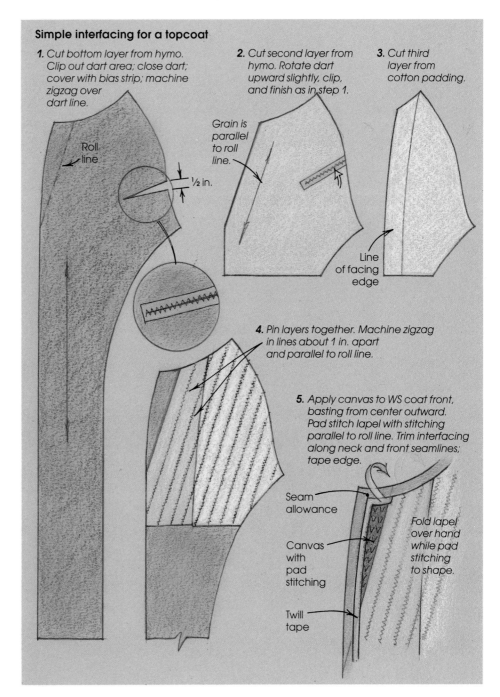

Simple interfacing for a topcoat

1. Cut bottom layer from hymo. Clip out dart area; close dart; cover with bias strip; machine zigzag over dart line.

Roll line

½ in.

2. Cut second layer from hymo. Rotate dart upward slightly, clip, and finish as in step 1.

Grain is parallel to roll line.

3. Cut third layer from cotton padding.

Line of facing edge

4. Pin layers together. Machine zigzag in lines about 1 in. apart and parallel to roll line.

5. Apply canvas to WS coat front, basting from center outward. Pad stitch lapel with stitching parallel to roll line. Trim interfacing along neck and front seamlines; tape edge.

Seam allowance

Canvas with pad stitching

Fold lapel over hand while pad stitching to shape.

Twill tape

marized steps and techniques found in basic tailoring texts to save room for the details you may not be able to find.

Planning seams—Before I cut out the pattern pieces from coat fabric, I carefully checked the kind of seams I'd need; all the seams were either flat fell or plain. I allowed ¾ in. for flat-fell seams (center back, shoulder to wrist, sides), so I could fold one seam allowance over and under the other trimmed one, and ½ in. for the plain seams (sleeve underarms, facings, neckline, armscyes). The side seams fell to the back, the sleeves to the front, and the center back fells to the left. I also allowed 1½ in. for the bottom hem.

Cut out the main coat pieces—fronts,

backs, sleeves, facings—and mark the location of the pockets, hemlines, interfacing, and lining. If you're going to add the undercollar and top collar following a classic tailoring technique, you need not cut those pieces out yet, since they are shaped to fit. Otherwise, follow your pattern instructions.

Camouflage pocket cover—Adding coat-fabric pocket covers is a way to clean finish the inside of a coat when it has a half lining. Since it's easier to work on small parts of the coat, I added the welt pockets to the coat fronts before I stitched the side or shoulder seams. If you have a welt pocket pattern, follow the directions and add pockets now; they need not be double-entry. If you want to add a double-entry pocket, one is explained in detail in the article on pp. 20-25.

After you have the pockets in place, cut a pocket cover for each pocket, referring to the shape and general dimensions shown in the pattern schematic on p. 77. The forward part of each pocket will be covered by the facing; this is why the shape of the actual pocket is not the same as the pocket cover. The cover must be bigger than the pocket by at least ¾ in. along the bottom and the curve so you can attach the lining strip and still have room for the pocket underneath to expand. It extends above the lining hem about 1 in. and stops about ½ in. into the facing. It's better to have the cover a bit too big than too small. Add the bias lining strip as shown in the drawing sequence on p. 78, and fell the bias to the coat. Anchor the cover to the pocket by stitching in the ditch at the ends of the welt through all layers.

Hair canvas interfacing—I've never seen a published description of an interfacing like the one Hostek showed me for a topcoat (see the construction sequence on p. 79). Two of the three interfacing layers—the hair canvas ones closest to the coat—are shaped slightly by a dart that points to the broadest part of the chest. (If your pattern doesn't call for shaping, just cut the interfacing using your pattern.) The clever part is that the darts don't coincide; the dart is rotated slightly up in the second interfacing layer to reduce bulk. A topcoat interfacing normally has no sharp, precise roll line; I drew one in anyway, from the top of the

next-to-top button to the neckline, about 3 in. from the front edge.

Cut two pieces of hymo with the grain positioned as shown. Cut the cotton padding so it falls just inside the facing line—the padding doesn't have a dart; you'll just trim it to size later.

Trim the darts from the hair canvas, butt the edges, and set them in place by machine zigzagging a strip of lining over the edges. Layer all three interfacings, smaller layers on top, and machine zigzag them together into a panel; the interfacing is now ready to baste to the coat as described in standard tailoring texts.

Working with the right side of the coat facing you and the interfacing panel underneath (smallest layer bottom-most), pin and baste the interfacing to the wrong side of the fronts with long stitches through all layers, working from the center outward. The important point is to make sure the coat fabric lies smooth against the interfacing, without bubbles or ripples. Be sure to permanently catch-stitch the pocket and the pocket cover to the interfacing to hold them in place when the basting is removed; do this by folding back the coat (right sides together) until a portion of the pocket is exposed for stitching.

With interfacing basted to the coat, I pad stitched the "lapel" area (see *Basics*, No. 38, p. 14). To give it shape, I folded the front upper corner over my hand as I stitched. I trimmed the canvas to just inside the facing seamline at the front and neck edges so it wouldn't add bulk in the seam, and I twill-taped the front edge and a section of the hem so it wouldn't stretch, just inside the seamline (this is a

standard technique).

Now baste on and machine stitch the facing. Then add vertical breast pockets in the facings (if you desire) as described in tailoring texts. It's also the time to bind the facings' raw edges below the level of the half-lining hem with lining strips, using the same technique described for the pocket cover. You'll fell the second edge of the lining strip to the coat after positioning the half lining.

A back with a lined vent—Join the two back pieces with a flat-fell seam, stopping at the top of the vent. Line the vent as shown in the drawing below.

Construct the sleeves, using a flat-fell seam for the shoulder-to-wrist seam, and a plain seam for under the arm. Finish the sleeve hems and insert the sleeve linings, tacking them to the sleeves along the underarm seam in several places to hold them in place, wrong sides together.

Half lining—Before attaching the sleeves, prepare the half lining for the fronts and backs. Cut rectangles of heavy lining fabric larger than the area of the fronts and backs, as shown in the drawing on p. 77; hem the bottoms, but don't trim the armscye and side seam shapes.

Pin and baste the front linings to the facings, right sides together, from neckline to hem, then machine stitch. Press the seam allowances toward the lining, then turn the lining right side out. Baste the lining to the front to hold it in place, making sure it isn't tight, or pulling on the coat. Roughly trim the extra lining from the neckline and armscyes, but leave generous seam allowances.

Next, stitch the two back lining rectangles together along the center back, and hem it to match the front linings. Baste the lining to the back along the center seam only, folding in a ½-in. pleat at center back. Roughly trim around the armscyes and neckline. Then stitch the side seams together with flat-fell seams.

Inset the sleeves using plain seams (leave the linings free). For strength and stability, I taped the entire armscye seam as I basted the sleeves in, then machine stitched the seam. Finally, I topstitched on the coat ½ in. along the armscye seams to about 8 in. down from the neckline front and back to match the flat-fell stitching lines of the side seams.

With sleeves in place and the neckline seam complete, I could begin the collar.

A convertible collar

I've come across a discussion of convertible collar construction only once, in an old tailoring book from early this cen-

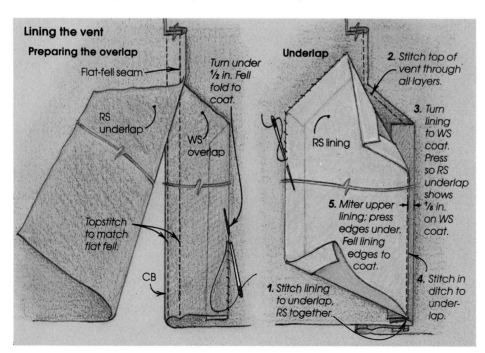

Lining the vent

Preparing the overlap

Flat-fell seam

RS underlap

Turn under ½ in. Fell fold to coat.

WS overlap

Topstitch to match flat fell.

CB

Underlap

RS lining

2. Stitch top of vent through all layers.

3. Turn lining to WS coat. Press so RS underlap shows ⅛ in. on WS coat.

5. Miter upper lining; press edges under. Fell lining edges to coat.

1. Stitch lining to underlap, RS together.

4. Stitch in ditch to underlap.

tury, so I was particularly curious to hear from Hostek how it's done. It turns out to be a clever bit of tailoring, which is described below and shown in the drawing sequence at right. My coat's collar was applied entirely by hand; only the preparation of the undercollar is presented here since application to the coat, and the addition of the top collar, is described in tailoring texts.

So how do you create two roll lines on a single collar? The answer is to make the lower one in the usual way—by pad stitching the shaping into the undercollar as you attach the linen—but to cut the interfacing along the upper roll line, creating a weak area where the collar will naturally bend when the coat is buttoned to the neck.

The collar linen is cut larger than the undercollar and on bias, and the seam is offset slightly from the undercollar's.

Finishing—Before felling the sleeve linings to the half lining of the coat, permanently stab-stitch the body linings to the armscye seam allowances. Then slip-stitch the lining's side seams together.

Add the top collar. Then stitch in the ditch along the entire neckline through all layers, making tiny invisible stitches by hand with a doubled thread, and fell the neck edge over the lining.

Now make the buttonholes, but practice on scrap fabric first. I used the standard method described in tailoring texts (a hand-worked buttonhole is described in *Threads*, No. 37, p. 14), except I doubled the size F thread so the size of the purls of the hand-worked buttonhole stitches would match the scale of the coat, and I used zigzag stitches to outline the buttonhole before slashing open the buttonhole for hand stitching. When you add the buttons, back each with a plain button on the inside for extra strength.

Machine topstitch the front edges and around the collar at ½ in. Fell the bias-bound facing edges to the coat, and the front lining hems to the top edge of the pocket cover. Finish the edge of the coat hem with bias that matches the facing bias. Blindstitch the hem to the coat.

Traditionally, men's overcoats have a large label at the bottom of the lining at center back; I'm just now considering what to put there, if anything. It seems that such a major project deserves an emblem of some kind, but the enormous satisfaction of wearing the coat will probably be enough. ☐

David Page Coffin is an associate editor of Threads. *He is currently preparing the expanded version of his custom shirt book.*

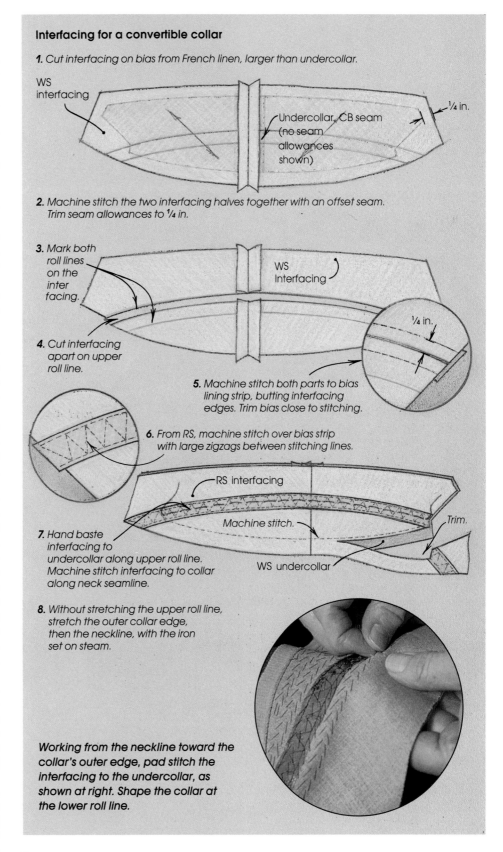

Interfacing for a convertible collar

1. *Cut interfacing on bias from French linen, larger than undercollar.*

WS interfacing

Undercollar, CB seam (no seam allowances shown)

¼ in.

2. *Machine stitch the two interfacing halves together with an offset seam. Trim seam allowances to ¼ in.*

3. *Mark both roll lines on the interfacing.*

WS Interfacing

¼ in.

4. *Cut interfacing apart on upper roll line.*

5. *Machine stitch both parts to bias lining strip, butting interfacing edges. Trim bias close to stitching.*

6. *From RS, machine stitch over bias strip with large zigzags between stitching lines.*

RS interfacing

Machine stitch.

Trim.

WS undercollar

7. *Hand baste interfacing to undercollar along upper roll line. Machine stitch interfacing to collar along neck seamline.*

8. *Without stretching the upper roll line, stretch the outer collar edge, then the neckline, with the iron set on steam.*

Working from the neckline toward the collar's outer edge, pad stitch the interfacing to the undercollar, as shown at right. Shape the collar at the lower roll line.

Sources for tailoring supplies

Greenberg & Hammer, Inc.
24 West 57th St.
New York, NY 10019
(800) 955-5135; (212) 246-2835
Catalog upon request;
$10 minimum order.

B. Black & Sons
548 S. Los Angeles St.
Los Angeles, Ca 90013
(213) 624-9451
Price list upon request;
$30 minimum order

Safari for the City

A simply sewn jacket from prints you quilt yourself

by Linda Faiola

everyone is headed for the country, judging by the clothes walking the streets these days. Topping off a pair of athletic leggings is often a billowy, gathered-waist anorak, the likes of which the wilderness has never seen. Even Oscar de la Renta has leaped to the rugged look with a jacket in brightly colored printed and quilted silk.

Although the pattern companies have heeded the outdoor trend by including anoraks and parkas in their catalogs, commercially quilted fabrics can't match the gorgeous ones that the fashion designers are using. Why not consider quilting a fabric of your choice?

Over the last 20 years I've made somewhere between 25 and 30 quilted jackets in assorted styles. A few are one color, but many more, like the jackets shown at right, are made from prints. You can have wonderful fun creating unique materials by quilting on multicolored, patterned textiles by hand or machine. Best of all, prints hide all sorts of sin, so your quilting doesn't have to be perfect.

Let the fabric be your inspiration and keep the jacket construction simple. The batting and backing that add loft and dimension to the quilting can hide the stitches of hemlines that you might worry about in a single-layer garment. Seams can be neatly bound so the inside of the jacket looks as neat as the outside. I'll give you some ideas for playing with the quilting design, and how to quilt by hand or machine, along with ways to hide buttonholes and to insert a pocket so you don't have to weaken a seam with clipping.

From *Threads* magazine (August 1991) 36:54-59

A jacket made from printed fabric you quilt at home can be exotic and hand quilted (left), or knock-around and machine quilted (right). Select a jacket pattern with few seams, and apply the tips for seams, pockets, and buttons as suggested by the author to keep jacket construction clean and simple. (Both jackets by Linda Faiola, hand-painted silk jungle fabric by Iren Rothenberger, photo by Yvonne Taylor)

Preplanning

Quilted jacket styles are not limited to anoraks; any loose jacket or coat pattern is worth consideration. Just be aware that garments with excessive seams are inappropriate choices since the seam allowances add stiffness and bulk.

Considering how much time you'll spend quilting the fabric, it's wise to make a muslin test garment to check fit and shape; you're going to quilt only the amount of fabric you really need in blocks that fit each pattern piece. Make any length and width adjustments to sleeves and body pieces.

Check the sewing details and decide which ones you might simplify. Do you want to bind the hem edges or turn them up? Bound edges require only a seam allowance.

Supplies

The shell fabric, batting, and backing must work well together, so it pays to match them carefully.

Before you buy or cut fabric, ask yourself a few questions. Will you wear the jacket only for special occasions or do you want something wonderful for every day? Why not make jackets you can wear every day, rather than ones that will hang in the closet most of the time.

How are you going to care for the jacket? Do you want to be able to machine wash it or do you prefer to dry-clean it? Are you willing to hand wash it?

If you are going to hand or machine wash the jacket, launder the yardage exactly as you will launder the finished garment. If you are uncertain of washability, cut a fabric swatch and test it; an advantage to sewing your own clothes is being able to choose and prepare fabrics specifically for home washing. The batting may need preshrinking, too; follow instructions on the package.

Shell fabric—As you shop for shell fabric, try to imagine if you'll still like the fabric by the time you finish the jacket. This may sound strange, but since you'll be spending lots of time quilting, you had better like the fabric a lot.

Quilting is best and most easily worked on lightweight, smooth fabrics. I prefer the touch and feel of natural fibers, which also breathe when worn. For a light jacket, try a silk or cotton. Both come in a variety of solid

Harmonious quilting patterns for whimsical fabrics: Hey, diddle, diddle fiddles for cows; geometrics for cartoon cats; and grapes and vines for a kitchen garden theme.

colors, prints, weights, and textures.

Silk has wonderful qualities. It is extremely luxurious and lightweight, is available in brilliant colors, and can be affordable. Thanks to mail order, it is available to everyone. Silk's major disadvantage is that not all types can be hand washed and some can be difficult to work with. If you're considering silk and aren't sure how it will handle, buy a small amount and try quilting it; wash a swatch in cold water with a mild soap like Ivory dishwashing liquid. Rough fingertips will catch and snag silk, so it is helpful to have one's fingers as smooth as possible. If the silk color runs, you'll have to dry-clean the jacket.

Working with hand-painted crepe de chine silk was a pleasant experience, even though this was the first time I hand quilted silk. One unexpected bonus was finding that I could roll the jacket up, stuff it in a bag, and shake out the wrinkles when I took it out of the bag to wear.

Cotton is a wonderful, all-purpose fabric. It's easy to work with, available everywhere, and is usually washable by hand or machine. Cotton can be as beautiful as many types of silk.

One of the best places in a fabric store to look for fun or whimsical cotton fabric is the children's department. I've found some wonderful cotton prints.

Backing—I prefer not to use a separate lining in a quilted garment since I want the stitches in the backing to show. Try a smooth, soft, lightweight cotton, such as batiste—sometimes called cotton sheath lining—or lawn. Although cotton broadcloth, a typical quiltmaking fabric, is stiff, heavy,

and rough compared to batiste, it is readily available in a wide range of colors, and is acceptable to use. Printed or monotone Liberty of London cottons also make light, smooth backings. Muslin turns into a soft, easy-to-work, suitable backing fabric after being washed, and it can be dyed.

Batiste and lawn are becoming hard to find, but check mail-order sources for French or heirloom sewing supplies, which often have pastel colors or white.

Batting—Batting affects the look and feel of the final jacket. Fiber batts come in 100% cotton, cotton/polyester blends, 100% polyester, and 100% wool. You can also consider a woven fabric such as cotton flannel or a soft wool interlining made to pad overcoats.

The choice of batting also affects the size, ease, and speed of hand or machine quilting. Most importantly, it determines the amount of quilting necessary to hold the layers together through years of wearing and laundering. Before deciding on the type of batting to use, you have to decide on how much quilting you are willing to do.

Cotton batting requires closely spaced lines of stitching to hold it securely to the shell and backing to prevent shrinking. Some say the lines of stitches should be no farther apart than 1 in. to avoid clumping and severe wrinkles when the jacket is washed. I usually quilt cotton with rows of stitching $\frac{1}{4}$ in. to $\frac{3}{8}$ in. apart. There are new 100% cotton batts on the market that are supposed to require less stitching than the older cotton batts require.

Batting that is part cotton and part polyester holds together with fewer stitches. Fairfield Processing's 80% cotton/20% polyester

"Cotton classic" gives good results, particularly when preshrunk according to the directions included in the package.

By hand or machine

Quilting will be the most time-consuming part of making the jacket, so choose wisely between hand and machine quilting. Here are some observations on both methods:

Hand quilting is relaxing and portable. Quilting curves and angles is easy, and the hand stitches produce a softer, more drapable fabric than machine stitching. Hand stitches are looser than machine stitching, so you won't want to stitch outside a pattern's cutting lines where you'll only have to cut away the fabric. You have to plan your quilting carefully, which I describe below.

Machine quilting is faster than hand quilting and is terrific for lots of straight lines on grain. Machine quilting can be awkward when working on large pieces; the smaller the piece, the easier it is to quilt. Since it is locked more firmly into the fabric, machine stitching can be cut if it's near an edge that will get stitched into a seam. However, machine stitches can dramatically change the feel of fabric, making it stiffer than hand quilting. Sometimes the stiffness is desirable.

Some people are very critical and picky about the size and perfection of hand quilting, or the exactness of machine stitching, but I say, relax, have fun, and don't worry about perfect stitching. People will notice the overall harmony of your jacket design, quilting, and print and won't have time to examine your stitches minutely. The greatest part of your creative time should be spent thinking of quilting patterns that work with the fabric. My quilting pattern ideas for three prints from my stash of fabrics are shown at left.

How do you decide whether to use hand or machine quilting, or select a pattern? Try them out. Layer the shell on top of the batting and backing and see what works. See what looks right. I tested the crepe de chine with different batting and stitches before I decided on hand stitching and a cotton/poly batt.

A sample will also tell you how much the fabric will shrink from the gathering effect of the quilting. The more quilting you do, the more shrinkage you'll get. Wasting some fabric is unavoidable in a project like this, so be sure to buy extra fabric.

Layout for hand quilting

Using the pattern as a guide, cut a piece of the shell fabric several inches longer and several inches wider than the pattern piece. Also cut identically sized layers of batting and backing.

Remember to cut mirror images for patterns such as sleeves and fronts. Quilting is easier if the grainlines of the shell and backing fabric match, so observe the pattern and fabric grainlines when cutting the pieces.

Working on a table, preferably one that does not have a slippery surface, sandwich the layers. Spread the backing right side down, spread the batting over the backing, and place the shell layer over the backing, right side up (see drawing sequence, right).

If the fabrics are slippery, pin the layers together to keep them from sliding around; long pins with highly visible plastic or glass heads are helpful. (If working on silk, make sure your needles and pins are sharp and have no burrs.)

Baste the sandwich together with stitches about 1½ in. to 2 in. long. Try not to lift the fabric with your hands, which will cause the layers to misalign. Use backstitches to lock the thread ends in place.

For quilting, you can use a hoop just as you would when making a quilt (I wouldn't recommend this for silk). I find small pieces easier to handle without the hoop. Begin in the middle of the piece working out in all directions. If the basting stitches get in the way, clip them.

Regularly place the pattern over the sandwich to see how close the quilting is getting to the cutting lines. When the quilting is within 3 in. or 4 in. of the cutting lines, pin the pattern piece to the sandwich and outline the pattern shape with basting. Continue quilting towards the outline, which is only a temporary guide since the quilting will shrink the fabric.

When the quilting is within an inch of the basting, remove the basting, repin the pattern to the sandwich, and rebaste the outline with short stitches that go through all layers. Finish the quilting, stopping just short of the cutting line by about ⅛ in.

With short running stitches, stitch through all the layers about ⅛ in. inside the cutting line. Pin the pattern to the sandwich for one last check, then cut the shape.

Quiet stitching

In your hand quilting, try for evenly spaced stitches about ⅛ in. long. The thicker the batt, the harder it is to make short stitches. If you can't make even, small stitches, don't let it stop you from making a quilted garment. Stitches that are ¼ in. long work fine.

For most quilting, I recommend 100% cotton quilting thread, available in many colors; quilting thread is thicker and stronger than regular sewing thread. If I need small amounts of additional colors, I use 100% cotton sewing thread which I wax lightly with beeswax. Try different needles to see which one works best for your selection of fabric and batting; for instance, I found that a No. 9 sharp needle (see *Basics*, No. 36,

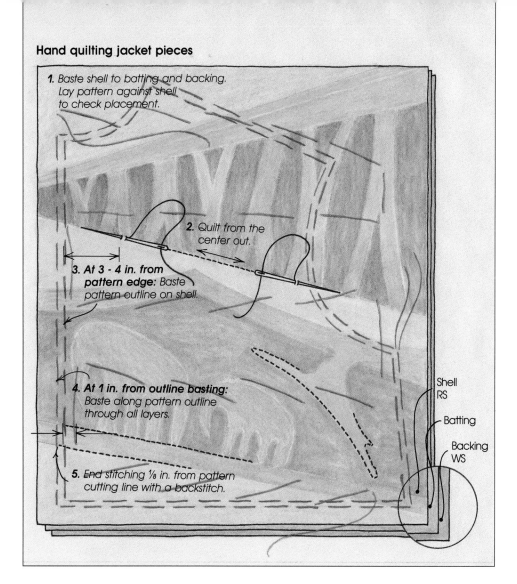

Hand quilting jacket pieces

1. Baste shell to batting and backing. Lay pattern against shell to check placement.

2. Quilt from the center out.

3. At 3 - 4 in. from pattern edge: Baste pattern outline on shell.

4. At 1 in. from outline basting: Baste along pattern outline through all layers.

5. End stitching ⅛ in. from pattern cutting line with a backstitch.

Shell RS

Batting

Backing WS

pp. 16 and 18) was easier to pull through silk fabric than a between, which I usually use with the fabric under tension in a hoop.

To quilt without a hoop, I pinch the fabric sandwich with my left hand and move it up and down with a seesaw motion into the tip of the needle, the eye of which is supported by a thimble on my right middle finger (left photo, next page). The thimble on my left hand underneath the sandwich tends to blunt the needle, which makes it hard to push through the fabric, so I change needles frequently, particularly when working with silk.

It helps to work with several threads and needles, moving them all gradually away from the center of the piece (drawing above). If you find working with several needles awkward, pull the needles off and rethread them as needed. Start the threads, each about 15 in. to 18 in. long, with a stitch near or in the middle of the fabric. Leaving a tail half the thread length, take one or two small backstitches to lock the thread. When you've finished quilting toward one edge, go back to the tail, thread it onto a needle, and quilt in the other direction. End threads with backstitches;

pass the needle through the layers, surfacing the needle about 1 in. away. Pull the thread gently and cut the tail slightly away from the surface; the thread should pull into the fabric and disappear as it springs back from the tension.

If I have enough thread on the needle and need to "jump" to another area, I pass the needle through the layers. This way I avoid ending one thread and beginning another.

Secure machine quilting

You might think that machine quilting is a breeze, but you need to set aside plenty of time. Quilting a square foot of fabric with machine-stitched rows spaced ¼ in. to ⅜ in. apart takes about an hour. I don't find machine quilting at all relaxing, but it has its advantages, including that the sandwich doesn't need basting prior to quilting. Basting would only get caught on the presser foot. This method works well for pieces up to 32 in. long and 36 in. wide.

Close rows of machine stitching will shrink the sandwich more than wide rows or hand quilting. To gauge shrinkage, carefully measure the first piece you quilt before and after quilting. ⇨

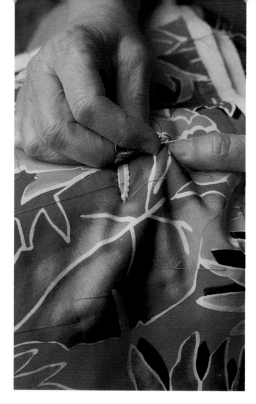

Quilting by hand or machine: Hand quilting (shown at left) is a contemplative lap activity. Faiola supports the needle's eye with a thimble on her right hand. She manipulates the fabric into the needle tip with her left hand.

Machine quilt blocks of fabric by carefully feeding the fabric into the needle with both hands (photo at right). Loose basting stitches keep the quilt roll neat and out of the way; chalked lines are references for approximately parallel stitching.

Cut a rectangle of shell fabric, batting, and backing, leaving extra all around as described for hand quilting. Lay the sandwich flat on the table, and mark the location of the first row of stitching with a ruler and tailors' chalk or a sliver of *white* bath soap that has developed a sharp edge. Use a long ruler to get perfectly straight lines; don't move a short ruler to mark a distance greater than the ruler's length. Don't use wax for marking; it can stain your fabric. Using the first line as a reference, draw parallel lines every 2 in. to one side of the first line. Pin the layers together on the marked side of the line. Roll up the other side and baste to keep it in place (right photo above).

Wind a lot of bobbins; due to the nature of a sewing machine, you'll go through more bobbin thread than top thread.

Use your hands to keep the layers feeding evenly into the needle. Machine stitch along the first line. Lift the presser foot and pivot the fabric, then machine stitch back, using the presser foot as a guide. Remove the pins as you come to them; *never* sew over pins. Continue stitching up and down, judging by eye how parallel to the guidelines the stitching lines are.

Roll up the machine-stitched side as it grows to keep it out of the way. After you've finished stitching that half of the fabric, unroll, smooth out, and lightly press the unstitched side. Roll the stitched side and repeat the process to finish the other half.

If you machine stitch with a contrasting color thread, then your stitching should be very even or deliberately uneven. If your stitching isn't as good as you'd like it to be, then use a matching color thread.

The easy part

Quilted garment construction is relatively easy compared to the quilting. Plan to avoid tailoring techniques such as interfacings, bound buttonholes, welt pockets, and free-hanging linings to reduce construction to its simplest form.

Seam finishes—Since there's no lining, the garment should be finished as nicely on the inside as on the outside. Binding the seams after machine stitching is my choice for the best finish. I find it unnecessary to remove batting from the seam allowances, which would be difficult since the quilting stitches extend into the seam allowances.

Cut binding strips—on bias for curved seams and on the crossgrain for straight seams—from either scraps of shell fabric or backing fabric. Crossgrain can be quite elastic and is easy to handle. I use strips 1 in. to 1½ in. wide for binding. Try a few widths to see what works for you.

There are many ways to bind a seam. The finish I frequently use is to press both seam allowances to one side, stitch one edge of the binding to the raw edges of both seam allowances at the same time, fold the binding over the allowances to cover them, and fell stitch the binding to the backing by hand (photo, facing page).

Before pressing seams, test your technique—pressing seams with your fingers may work better than pressing with an iron. After pressing the first seam in the silk jacket, for example, I decided that I didn't like the resulting textured silk. Instead, I pinched the seam allowances open with my fingers and pinned them in place while I attached the binding.

An unclipped pocket—The instructions in commercial patterns usually call for you to stitch the pocket front and back to their respective garment seam allowances, and then to stitch the garment side seam; the stitching breaks on each side of the pocket opening. To press the pocket toward the front, you are told to clip the seam allowance below the pocket opening. I have devised a pocket that doesn't require any clipping; the seam allowances are pressed open and then bound to the front and back of the jacket backing, as shown in the left-hand drawings and the photo on the facing page.

Buttonholes—I decided to use buttons and buttonholes for the closure on the silk jacket, and frankly, the buttonholes gave me the most grief of any of the details. The more reasonable option would have been to use a fly facing that has a hidden buttonhole placket, like the one shown in the right-hand drawings on the facing page. The facing would have been unquilted, the buttonholes could be put in before the facing was applied, and—most importantly—if I made a mistake, I could make a new buttonhole placket.

You can use this same hidden placket in sweaters or for any garment on which you don't want the buttons and the buttonholes to show. The placket can also be made out of grosgrain. □

Linda Faiola is a professional pattern-maker and machine knitter who teaches classes in quilting, knitting, and garment construction at the Cambridge Center for Adult Education in Cambridge, MA.

Sewing an unclipped pocket

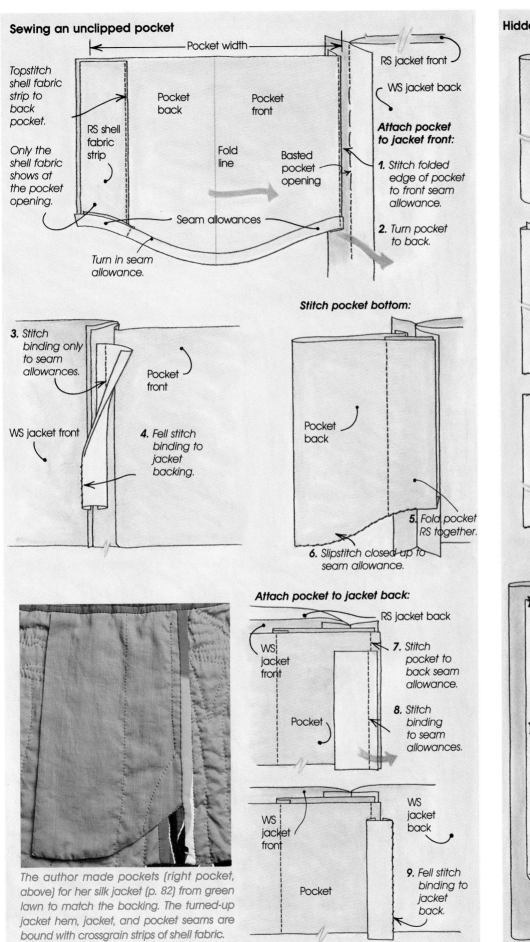

Topstitch shell fabric strip to back pocket.

Only the shell fabric shows at the pocket opening.

Pocket width

RS shell fabric strip

Pocket back

Pocket front

Fold line

Basted pocket opening

RS jacket front

WS jacket back

Turn in seam allowance.

Seam allowances

Attach pocket to jacket front:

1. Stitch folded edge of pocket to front seam allowance.

2. Turn pocket to back.

3. Stitch binding only to seam allowances.

Pocket front

WS jacket front

4. Fell stitch binding to jacket backing.

Stitch pocket bottom:

Pocket back

5. Fold pocket RS together.

6. Slipstitch closed up to seam allowance.

Attach pocket to jacket back:

RS jacket back

WS jacket front

Pocket

7. Stitch pocket to back seam allowance.

8. Stitch binding to seam allowances.

WS jacket front

Pocket

WS jacket back

9. Fell stitch binding to jacket back.

The author made pockets (right pocket, above) for her silk jacket (p. 82) from green lawn to match the backing. The turned-up jacket hem, jacket, and pocket seams are bound with crossgrain strips of shell fabric.

Hidden buttonhole placket

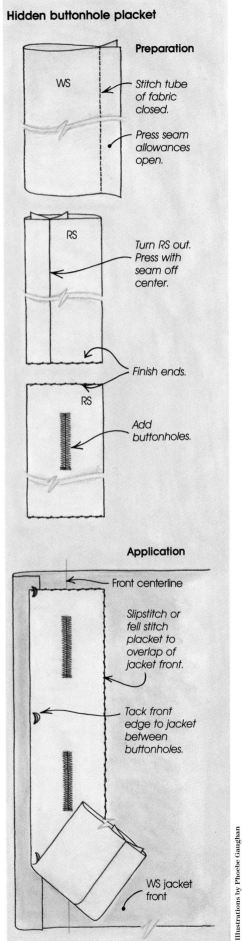

Preparation

WS

Stitch tube of fabric closed.

Press seam allowances open.

RS

Turn RS out. Press with seam off center.

Finish ends.

RS

Add buttonholes.

Application

Front centerline

Slipstitch or fell stitch placket to overlap of jacket front.

Tack front edge to jacket between buttonholes.

WS jacket front

Illustrations by Phoebe Gaughan

The Incredible, Reversible, One-Technique Jacket

Machine quilting as a construction method

by Bird Ross

a friend once said to me, "Make your work look as good on the inside as it does on the outside." Little did I realize then what an impact that advice would have on the things I make now, almost 10 years later. My work, like the tops and hats on the facing page, has no right or wrong side; it's double-sided, completely reversible, and I get to play with at least twice as much color and pattern as I would if I were making only one-sided pieces.

I construct each of my garments without any of the usual construction techniques. They're entirely formed out of the randomly stitched machine quilting that I use to hold together the three layers: inside, outside, and a stabilizer in the middle. Using only the forward and reverse straight stitch on the most basic sewing machine (I have an old Singer Featherweight), I can join sections, finish seams and edges, and create texture and pattern, all at once. As I quilt the layers of fabric, I'm creating both sides of the jacket at the same time. I'm also transforming the colors and patterns of the commercial yardage by overlaying them with thread, and changing the effect of the cloth's original design by juxtaposing it with new patterns, as I add new fabrics.

There are three main steps to the process. First I choose a pattern and adapt it to my requirements. Then I select the two fabrics that I'll use inside and out in addition to an inner fabric, cut them out in identical layers, and machine quilt them together, covering the fabric with random lines of colored quilting. Finally, I

Bird Ross reinvents the garment by discarding everything she ever learned about sewing (well, almost). Her completely reversible, machine-washable pieces are constructed entirely with machine quilting. (Photo by Susan Kahn)

form the seams, finish the edges, and add pockets if I want them, in each case by machine quilting single layers of contrasting fabrics over the layered garment pieces. The process uses lots of thread!

I use the same techniques to create baskets, as well as hats, vests, and neckties. Machine quilting gives a whole new look and feel to the original fabric, and the juxtaposition of the patterns adds another intriguing element to the creation of garments. Here's how it's done.

Simplifying the pattern

I begin my garments with commercial patterns. I make sure to start with one whose basic shape excites me, since I'll be paring it down to the bare essentials. The patterns that work best are simple and uncluttered to begin with, without separate sleeve pieces. My jackets aren't meant to be fitted, and because of their bulk and relative stiffness (about the same as any heavily quilted garment), they'll be more comfortable if they're slightly oversized. If you've chosen a pattern that you've used before, the fit will be slightly less subtle because of the bulk and because you'll be eliminating some of the seams.

First adjust the pattern for size, then look for seams that you can do without. If the garment has a center-back seam, copy the pattern and tape the back pieces together to make a new pattern piece without the center seam, removing any shaping so the new pattern lies flat. You won't need any facings. I integrate separate collar pieces into the main pattern shape. If the sleeves have separate cuffs, simply lengthen the sleeves to incorporate the cuff length. I always add an extra two inches to each of the sleeves anyway to allow for shrinkage. It's easier to cut the length off later than it is to add length, and this way you can relax when you put the pieces in the washing machine. You

can use the pattern's patch pocket shapes when you make pockets later, or you can draw your own, but cut off any pockets that extend from the side seams.

Creating a new fabric

This technique lends itself to lots of variations, and the main variable is the feel and look of the new fabric you'll be creating by quilting layers. I've worked out some guidelines to help reduce your trial and error, but experimentation is part of the fun of the project, and I do lots of it. For a finished jacket with the least number of unpleasant surprises, it's vital that you make samples first so that you can check for color fastness and shrinkage. I usually make my jackets completely machine washable and dryable, but even if you plan to dry-clean yours, the layering and quilting process can cause major transformations, including shrinkage.

Making samples—Once you've chosen your fabrics, or better yet *before* you have any idea what fabrics you ultimately want to use in your jacket, cut out some sample squares and try the process. If you don't make any samples first, your final garment will be a very risky business.

Start by cutting eight 8-in. squares. Use a variety of fabrics including novelty fabrics, silks, cottons of various weights, transparent fabrics, anything you like. Pair these fabrics for a total of four back-to-back squares wrong sides together as they would be in a finished garment.

Then choose a fabric for the middle layer. This is a stabilizer that allows you to use any type of fabric on either side of it. It adds needed body if you want to use two very lightweight fabrics, and it helps balance very different fabrics.

The stabilizer also adds bulk, which is why I like to wash the layers as many as three times before the jacket is complete. This gives it a more relaxed feel. I use

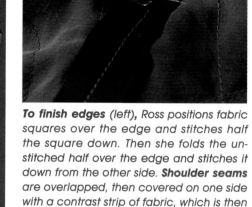

To finish edges (left), Ross positions fabric squares over the edge and stitches half the square down. Then she folds the unstitched half over the edge and stitches it down from the other side. **Shoulder seams** are overlapped, then covered on one side with a contrast strip of fabric, which is then zigzagged (above). On the other side, contrast fabric squares are zigzagged over the seam.

lightweight upholstery fabrics, such as chintzes, as stabilizers. They're all-cotton, 60 in. wide, and generally are available at larger fabric stores as bolt ends for very little money. Make sure the fabric won't bleed and that it's either a pale solid or a subtle print that won't show through.

Unless you're looking for the maximum texture (as described below), prewash this middle layer fabric. Cut four 8-in. squares and sandwich one between each of the four pairs of outer fabrics. Pin the three layers together using as few pins as you feel comfortable with. When you sew your jacket, you can use as many pins as you like to keep things from shifting. But on the sample, the fewer pins, the less to keep track of once you begin sewing.

Doing the manual zigzag—Remember when you were first learning to sew and you were told always to use the same color bobbin thread as the top thread, and that the thread should match your fabric? Well, forget those rules and pick your two favorite colors, ones that will complement, contrast, or conflict with the fabric in your first set of squares. Put one color on top and the other in your bobbin, and set your machine to sew a medium-length straight stitch.

Place your needle anywhere you want within the square. Lower the presser foot and begin by sewing several inches in one direction, then put your machine in reverse and sew backwards for several inches, without going over the original stitches, then again forwards and then again backwards. You're now doing what I call the "manual zigzag." It may take some practice before you get used to doing it with your machine. If yours is a machine

that requires you to hold the reverse button down as you sew in reverse, then practice until you feel comfortable holding the button and manipulating the fabric at the same time.

Do the manual zigzag randomly all over your 8-in. square. Try not to fill in any one area of your square more than another. Remove the pins as you get to them. Move all around the square with your machine, using just as many reverse as forward stitches. Don't be in a hurry. Think of these stitches as paint or colored pencil strokes, and add lots of color.

Sew all four samples separately, adding as much color as you like. You won't be completely covering the square with thread, but sew a greater concentration of stitches in some squares than others so that you'll get an idea of the various effects. You can try synthetic as well as cotton thread, and try mixing them in top and bobbin. Try some metallic threads. I usually change threads three times on top and bobbin before I'm through.

Once you've completed the samples, toss them in the washing machine, and then into the dryer, unless any of them include fabrics you wouldn't ordinarily put in the machine or if you don't intend to wash them once they're made into a jacket. Once they're totally dry, iron them flat.

Some of your squares will have lots of texture. Notice how much your squares have or haven't shrunk. Some of that has to do with the fiber content, but a lot of it has to do with the number of stitches you put in your fabric: more stitches, more shrinkage. Notice, too, how unsquare some of the pieces may have become, or how different layers in the square may

have raveled or shrunk more than other layers. Trim the edges as little as possible to straighten them.

The changes that take place in your samples will tell you how to prepare the fabric before you begin on your jacket. For example, if the fit of your garment would be spoiled if it shrinks, then prewash and dry all of your fabric layers twice to shrink the fabric as much as possible before you do any of the cutting and sewing. These preliminary washings will *not* keep the fabric from shrinking entirely because adding the stitches later will cause more shrinkage, but it helps.

Covering the edges—The next step for your sample is to cut about thirty-five 2-in. squares of contrasting fabric for each sample square. A rotary cutter and straightedge will be a big help. Position the squares to your right as you sit at the machine. Pick up one square at a time, and lay the diagonal along the edge of the sample so that half of each little square falls off, as in the left-hand photo above, then sew it down with more manual zigzags. Move around the layered edges, laying down new little squares and overlapping the points about 1 in., and sewing only half of each square to the sample. The other half will be folded over later, wrapping around to finish the edge. It's a good idea to make some samples with curved edges, too, so you can practice finishing shapes like necklines and curved jacket openings.

Once you've gone completely around all of your edges, turn the sample over and sew down all the other halves of the little squares. Make sure you pull them flush to the edge of the sample. Don't pin

Machine quilting large pattern shapes cut from three layers of fabric requires a wide table, room to move, and a wide-armed grip on the fabric. A machine that can be set to sew in reverse frees both of Ross's hands for maximum control.

these down in advance; you'll want to manipulate them as you go. You can baste them all in place with a single row of stitches first. The corners will be bulky, so trim away any excess fabric from the 2-in. square as you fold.

Now put all the sample squares in the washer and dryer to check once more for shrinkage and squareness. Again, some of the texture and crookedness can be ironed out. Press the pieces just to see what happens. If you were happier with the texture before you did the pressing, just throw the pieces back in the washer and dryer.

Planning ahead—To control the final texture of your new fabric, try these ideas.

For the *most* texture and a soft, worn hand, use any combination of the following: Choose only natural fiber fabrics. Prewash only those fabrics which will shrink a great deal, like gauzes. Use fabrics which have different fiber contents; for example, you'll get a lot of texture if you sandwich two layers of cotton around a polyester middle layer because of the inconsistent shrinkage. If your thread content is different from your fiber content, you'll get more texture than if you use matching thread.

For *less* texture, use any combination of the following: Prewash all of your fabric before cutting. Use all synthetic fabrics. Sew with fewer manual zigzag stitches when you're sandwiching the layers together. All fabric layers and thread should have the same fiber content.

The more samples you make, the more discoveries you'll make, and the more questions you'll have answered before you get to the jacket. You should also feel

as comfortable sewing in reverse as you do going forward before you plunge into jacket making.

Sewing the jacket

Start by choosing your fabrics, both outer layers and the stabilizing layer. You can choose the edge fabric(s) when you get to that step.

You'll be cutting three layers at a time, so you'll need a big cutting surface. Lay the fabric out with the bottom layer face down. The middle layer can be either side up, but the top layer will be right side up. Pin the pattern pieces on top catching all three layers, and cut all the layers at once. Ideally, you'll have one pattern piece for the back and one pattern piece for the front, which you'll use twice, making sure you flip it over so you don't cut two left fronts.

Quilting the layers—Once they've been cut out, pin the three layers together thoroughly so that they will be ready for sewing. This takes a lot of pins on every 2 to 3 in. Perhaps you're wondering why I don't first sew the three layers of fabric together and then cut out the pattern pieces. You can do that; in fact, if you want to be absolutely sure you get no shrinkage in the garment, you might want to sew the layers together, wash and dry them, and then cut the pattern pieces out. However, you'll be using much more fabric, you'll have more waste once you cut out, and initially you'll be handling much bigger pieces of fabric at the machine.

Now you're ready to sew the layers together. Proceed with these pieces as you did with your sample squares. The fabric will be more cumbersome, and you can't

hold it the way you do for normal sewing. And instead of sewing a few inches before changing direction, you'll sew for about 6 to 8 in. before switching. Take your time and sew carefully. It will be tricky to keep everything flat. If you're having trouble, stop and put in more stabilizing pins. If you've put in too many pins and you're worrying about breaking your needle, take some out. But be sure to sew over the entire pattern piece.

It's important to have a consistent amount of stitching—heavy, medium, or light—within each piece, and the same consistency in all the pieces of a single garment. Otherwise you will get uneven puckering and shrinkage, and an irregular texture, which might lead to seams not matching, lengths being different, and so on. This first layer of thread is the most painstaking. You're fixing all of your layers together at this point. After this you'll be able to add as much thread and color as you want without having to worry about everything staying flat. I still get glitches where the fabric catches in a fold, but I just live with them.

Once you've finished with your first layer of thread, change your threads on the top and bottom and add other colors. I always sew a total of three layers of thread. After you've completed all the pattern pieces, wash them in hot water and throw them in the dryer, then give them a good steam pressing.

Making seams—The next step is to sew the pattern pieces together. Don't trim any of the edges of the jacket, even if you get uneven layering or puckering. The unevenness will be averaged out when you start putting the seams together. Let's assume you're working with a pattern like the ones I use, with shoulder seams that begin at the right and left sides of the neck and go all the way to the wrist. Take the right-front pattern piece and pin it so that it overlaps the edge of the back pattern piece about ½ in. Pin the pieces together and then sew them together with a single straight seam going from one end to the other.

Before you do the other shoulder seam, cut a strip of contrasting, prewashed fabric that's a few inches longer than your seam and about ¾ in. wide. Sew this strip with a single line of straight stitch on top of the lapped seam on the side of the jacket you'll usually wear inside, then go back and do a manual zigzag across the strip to seal the seam, as I'm doing in the right-hand photo on the facing page. Turn the jacket over, change your thread, and cover the seam on the other side with an overlapping line of 2-in. squares. This cre-

Ross's patch pockets are reachable from both sides, because there's a slit at the pocket mouth, so you can get to the patch when it's worn on the inside. This partially completed pocket shows how the slit is finished and the pocket is attached with quilted squares. There's a finished pocket on the jacket shown on the facing page.

Making reversible pockets

1. Determine position of pocket opening, and mark it. Reinforce with manual zigzags, using extra stitches at ends.

2. Slit opening with X-Acto knife or rotary cutter. Pins at ends will prevent overcutting.

3. Seal both edges with fabric squares.

4. Make an oversized three-layer sandwich for each pocket patch. Quilt, finish top edge with fabric squares, and shrink. Trim to final size.

5. Position patch at slash, stitch around, and seal the seam with fabric squares.

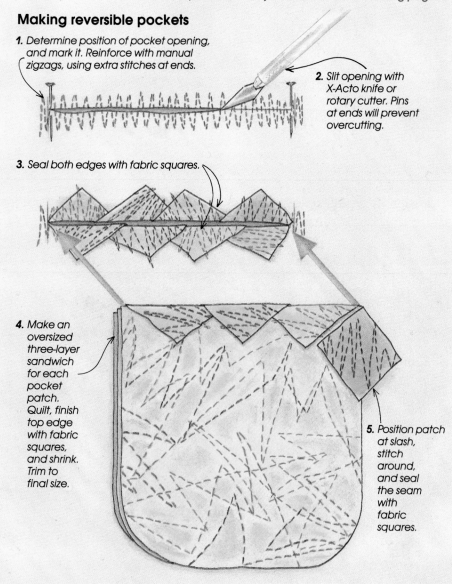

Illustration by Phoebe Gaughan

ates a diamond pattern from the neck to the wrist if you choose a contrast fabric, but it can be almost invisible if you use squares of the same fabric. Either way, cover the squares with more manual zigzag stitch, choosing new thread colors if you like. You are working with a total of eight layers of fabric here, so proceed cautiously. I recommend changing to a new or larger needle.

Once you've completed both shoulder seams, but before you tackle the underarm seam, it's time to finish the edges around the neck, down the front, and across the hem. This will be exactly like finishing the edges on your sample squares and circles. For the really tight curves around the neck, I sometimes use smaller squares because they're easier to shape. Then trim the sleeve ends even, but leave them a little long because they could still shrink a bit, and finish them with the 2-in. squares. For the last time before the jacket is complete, put it in the washer and dryer, then press it thoroughly before you sew the closing seams.

The underarm seams are very straightforward; they're the most like normal sewing of all the steps, because I use a regular right-sides-together seam, and bind it in the usual way. Sew the entire seam, then trim it to ¼ in. Cut two bias strips of contrast fabric 1½ in. wide and the length of one seam plus 2 in. With about 1 in. hanging off at each end, sew one strip right side down on top of the existing seamline with its edge aligned with the trimmed seam allowances. Backstitch at the ends of the seam, then fold the extra lengths back over the seam and turn the strip over the raw edges. You can fold the strip lengthwise to finish its edge, or leave it to be trimmed later; since it's bias, it won't ravel. Then catch it in place by stitching in the ditch next to the first seam.

Making pockets—If you decide to add patch pockets, they will be your last step. Try the jacket on in front of a mirror and check the placement visually. I don't recommend putting the pockets in the side seams because they're harder to get to, and they're not as interesting to look at. The patch pockets (see photo and drawing at left) are completely usable from both sides of the jacket, although the patch is only visible from one side. □

Bird Ross lives and maintains her studio in Madison, WI, where she is closing in on her MFA degree in sculpture. She exhibits her work internationally and was featured in the International Textile Competition in Japan this spring.

Whether you go bold or subtle, Ross's quick techniques for machine quilting reversible garments is a great way to explore wearable combinations of color and pattern.

Index